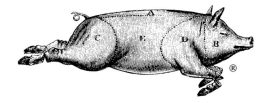

THE COMPLETE NOSE TO TAIL

FERGUS HENDERSON
JUSTIN PIERS GELLATLY

Photographs by Jason Lowe

BLOOMSBURY
LONDON · OXFORD · NEW YORK · NEW DELHI · SYDNEY

SEVEN THINGS
I SHOULD MENTION

When having lunch at Sweetings, you sit at a bar behind which
a waiter is trapped, you order your smoked eel, they yell to a runner
who delivers your eel over your shoulder to the waiter, who then
places it under the counter and then in front of you as if they had
it all along. Not an entirely practical way of getting your food,
but a splendid eating ritual, and a wonderful lunch.

'Nose to Tail Eating' means it would be disingenuous to the animal
not to make the most of the whole beast; there is a set of delights,
textural and flavoursome, which lie beyond the fillet.

This is a book about cooking and eating at home with friends
and relations, not replicating restaurant plates of food.

Do not be afraid of cooking, as your ingredients will know, and
misbehave. Enjoy your cooking and the food will behave; moreover
it will pass your pleasure on to those who eat it.

The perfect recipe manages to steady and uplift at the same time.

One afternoon my flat was broken into. The strange thing is, before
I went out I had put a hare in the oven to braise, which filled the flat
with delicious gamey smells. I cannot help but think that it must have
been very distracting to the burglar, the musk of a braising hare.

Unctuous potential: Trotter Gear is your gastronomic friend.

CONTENTS

SOMETHING TO GET THE JUICES
GOING AND PREPARE YOU
FOR LUNCH

CAMPARI AND WHITE WINE

I thought we should start this book with something to lead you into your indulgence, a cleansing glass to get the juices going. It's known in Italy as a bicyclette, as old men drink it and then wobble home on their bikes. Interestingly, Harry's Bar in Venice refuses to serve this concoction, rather as if it's Italy's version of a snakebite, but do not be deterred.

In a wineglass pour a measure of Campari, add some ice and top up with dry white wine. With trial and error, you shall find your chosen strength.

Your good health and appetite!

SOUP

(Never underestimate the power of Soup)

VEAL TAIL AND PEA SOUP

PUMPKIN AND BACON SOUP

PEA AND PIG'S EAR SOUP

FENNEL, BUTTER BEAN, OX TONGUE AND GREEN SAUCE

CHICKEN BROTH AND WILD GARLIC

NEW SEASON GARLIC AND BREAD SOUP

NETTLE AND SNAIL SOUP

POTATO AND BACK FAT SOUP

LEEK, POTATO AND OYSTER SOUP

ONION SOUP AND BONE MARROW TOAST

COCK-A-LEEKIE

VEAL TAIL
AND PEA SOUP

To serve four

veal bones, roasted in a hot oven
for half an hour

stock vegetables – carrot,
leek, celery, onion, garlic
– roughly chopped

a bundle of parsley, thyme and
a little rosemary

2 veal tails per person, brined for
at least a week (see page 269), then
a good soak in fresh water
overnight to desalinate

sea salt and black pepper

900g fresh peas in their pods,
podded just before use – or you
could apply the theory a wise chef
once told me, which was to use
fresh when peas are in season
and otherwise use frozen

This is a perfect case of why you must befriend your butchers and give them a bit of advance warning. They should be able to get you the tails. If they come in dribs and drabs, get your brine bucket out and use it as a holding tank until you have amassed enough tails.

Put the roasted veal bones, chopped stock vegetables and bundle of herbs into a pot. Place the tails on top, cover with water and simmer for 3 hours, skimming as you go. Then, using a sharp knife to make sure that the tails are thoroughly cooked, remove gently and put to one side.

Strain the broth and chill it thoroughly. Clarify the broth as described on page 267. Return to the heat and check the seasoning. Reintroduce the tails and, at the last moment, add the peas and serve.

Encourage the use of fingers in the picking up of the tails and giving them a good gnaw. This soup is a thing of beauty, with tails and peas bobbing about in a clear broth … Ahhh.

PUMPKIN AND BACON SOUP

Should easily serve twelve

3 onions, peeled

3 leeks, cleaned

5 peeled cloves of garlic

extra virgin olive oil

1kg piece of smoky streaky bacon, cubed or in chunks – keep skin in one piece

4 tinned tomatoes

1 pumpkin

3 bay leaves

a bundle of fresh thyme and parsley

at least 3.5 litres ham or chicken stock

sea salt and black pepper

A dish suitable for a large autumnal gathering. One pumpkin will feed many. For preference, choose an organic one, with a whitish/green skin that feels very hard; they are often available from health-food shops and some supermarkets.

Chop your onions, leeks and garlic. Put a good dose of olive oil into your pot, add the chopped vegetables and cook but do not brown. Add your chopped bacon and its skin. When these have released their fat, squish the tomatoes in your hands and add them, giving your dish a slight blush. Let all this cook down until you feel that they have really got to know each other, a gentle 25 minutes or so.

While this is happening, peel, seed and chop your pumpkin into approximately 2.5cm chunks. Add these and let them cook for about 5–10 minutes. Then add the bay leaves and the thyme and parsley bundle. Now add the stock, enough so that you end up with an Arctic Sea of soup with icebergs of pumpkin bobbing about in your broth. Simmer until the pumpkin is soft and giving, but not falling apart (though a little disintegration is not a bad thing), say 30–40 minutes. Season to taste and serve hot.

PEA AND PIG'S EAR SOUP

To serve four

1.5 litres flavoursome ham stock
(preferably the water you boiled
a ham in) or a ham bone
plus a head of garlic

500g green dried split peas, soaked
in water overnight and drained

2 pig's ears (ask your butcher, these
should not be hard to obtain; singe
off as much hair as you can)

2 whole white onions, peeled

sea salt and black pepper

vegetable oil for frying

This is based on a very dour recipe – dried peas, pig's ears and water, the ear giving a certain body to the soup – but it is no less delicious for that.

If you're using stock, bring it to the boil in a pan with the split peas, ears and onions, and then simmer until the peas are soft and cooked to a thick soupy consistency (approximately 3 hours). If it starts to get too thick add more stock or water. If you have a ham bone, just cover this with water, add your garlic, split peas, ears and onion, and cook the same way as with stock, though it will probably need some skimming. Add more water if it is getting too thick. Season to taste. Remove the onions and, if you have taken that route, the head of garlic and the ham bone.

Extract the ears from the soup, rinse them and dry them carefully. Allow them to cool and firm up, then slice very thinly. Heat vegetable oil in a deep frying pan (or deep fryer if you have one) and drop the ears in. Be careful, as even if dry they are likely to spit. Stir to avoid them sticking in one great mass. When crispy remove from the oil and lay on kitchen paper to drain off excess fat. Serve the soup hot. On top of each bowl place a cluster of crispy ear.

If you have any boiled ham left up your sleeve you could incorporate small chunks in your soup.

FENNEL, BUTTER BEAN, OX TONGUE AND GREEN SAUCE

Makes a pot that will do a hearty lunch for six

1 ox tongue, brined for 10–14 days (see page 269)

a few stock vegetables, such as carrot, leek, celery, onion, garlic, roughly chopped

extra virgin olive oil

6 heads of fennel, sliced thinly against the grain

4 firm white onions, peeled and sliced 3mm thick

8 cloves of garlic, peeled and left whole

1 small glass of Pernod

chicken stock

2 handfuls of butter beans, soaked overnight and then simmered thoroughly in clean water with a head of garlic, until they are soft, swollen pillows of joy (very important, as we know what happens to undercooked beans – nothing!)

sea salt and black pepper

Green Sauce (see page 255)

A lot going on for a soup, but what a soup!

Rinse the brined ox tongue and soak it for a couple of hours in fresh water. Put it in a pan with the stock vegetables, bring to the boil and simmer for 3 hours. Check with a knife; you want a thoroughly giving tongue. Peel it while still warm, then allow to cool.

We are almost ready to construct our soup … In a pot big enough to receive all the ingredients, pour a healthy splash of olive oil and put on a not too furious heat. Sweat off the fennel, onions and garlic until giving but not collapsing, as they still have some cooking to do. Add the Pernod.

At this point, add enough chicken stock to cover everything, then add the butter beans. What you want is beans *in* the soup, not a thick, beany soup. Think of the Mysterons of Captain Scarlet and the circles of light that came with them – that's the sort of bean ratio you are looking for in the soup. Let this simmer, allowing all the components to get to know each other.

Now slice as much tongue as you feel appropriate (keep the rest for sandwiches) into thin little angel's wings. Slip these into the soup. After a moment's more introductory simmering, check for seasoning and serve with a big bowl of Green Sauce to dollop, plus bread and wine.

A fine lunch.

CHICKEN BROTH
AND WILD GARLIC
To serve six

EITHER

*1 chicken (with the breast meat
and the flesh from the legs removed
and kept for the clarification) and
12 extra wings*

OR

*the liquor from a boiled chicken
you have eaten previously, and
2 extra chicken breasts*

2 peeled carrots

2 sticks of celery

2 peeled onions

2 leeks

1 whole head of garlic

*a bundle of bay, parsley, thyme
and rosemary*

black peppercorns

sea salt

*1 whole fresh chilli (optional, but
a good addition as if kept whole it
will give a subliminal warmth,
a mysterious 'wayhey')*

*a bundle of wild garlic (ramsons)
leaves, roughly chopped (you can
buy these in good greengrocers or
alternatively pick them yourself –
they are easy to spot due to their
pungent smell)*

**This is a very soothing, clear broth, ideal if you are feeling
a little frail.**

If you're using the chicken carcass, place the bones and wings in a
big pan and cover with water. Bring to the boil, skim off the scum,
and reduce to a simmer (a rolling boil churns the scum back into
the broth).

If you're using the liquor, start here.

Add your roughly chopped vegetables and herbs, seasoning, and
the chilli if using. Simmer for 2½ hours, skimming as necessary.
Strain, allow to cool and then clarify using the method on page 26.

Once you have your clear broth, reheat, meanwhile placing the garlic
leaves in the bottom of the soup bowl or bowls. Pour the hot soup over
these, give them a few moments to get to know each other, then eat.

NEW SEASON GARLIC AND BREAD SOUP

To serve six

8 fresh whole garlic heads

1 litre chicken stock

sea salt and black pepper

a healthy handful of chunks, without crust, of yesterday's – if not even the day before's – white bread

For the early months of spring you can get fresh garlic before it is dried. It has a longer, greener stem, giving you the flavour of garlic with a youthful nature. A mouli is very useful for this recipe – in fact a mouli is useful all the time.

Place the garlic in the stock and bring to the boil, then reduce to a simmer until the garlic is cooked soft – about 40 minutes. Then pass the garlic through the mouli (if you have no mouli, press it through a sieve). Mix the garlic pulp back into the stock and season to taste.

Reheat and throw in the bread a couple of minutes before serving, so it has just long enough to sup up the soup, but not fall apart.

NETTLE AND
SNAIL SOUP

To serve six

4 floury potatoes, peeled and
chopped into chunks

4 leeks, cleaned and sliced

2 onions, peeled and sliced

4 cloves of garlic, peeled
and chopped

extra virgin olive oil

1.5 litres light chicken stock

a good shopping bag full of nettles

SNAILS

24 fresh English snails, picked by
your fair hands (you will need
to put them in a bucket and let
them poo all their poo out for a few
days before cooking; then blanch in
boiling salt water, pull them
out of their shells and cook in a
court-bouillon – that is, water
with plenty of white wine and
flavoursome herbs – until tender);
or there is Tony the Snail Man,
who breeds snails (see right)

12 cloves of garlic, peeled and
finely chopped

a big knob of butter

sea salt and black pepper

This should be made with spring nettles, as by July they tend to take on a laxative quality. Probably not what you want from a soup.

In a saucepan sweat off all your chopped vegetables and garlic in olive oil, not browning them. This moment is important, as the more you can cook the vegetables at this point, the better the flavour of the soup. When the potatoes are cooked, add the stock. Let this all simmer, familiarizing the elements.

While still simmering away on the heat, add the nettles. Allow them to blanch for a moment – not long enough to lose their vivid green – then take off the heat and liquidize the lot.

At this point it might have a certain rustic, fibrous nature. Do not worry – you now need to pass the soup through a fine sieve twice, as eradicating any fibre somehow spiritually defeats the nettles by removing any fear of a tingle or a sting. You now hopefully have a green, silky soup.

Address your snails: pop the chopped garlic and butter into a heated frying pan. Allow for a little sizzle, then add the snails. Roll them around until piping hot, then season with salt and pepper.

Bowl up the nettle soup and spoon in 4 snails per person, which should stay on the top, sitting in a buttery, garlicky puddle.

P.S. Tony the Snail Man said I could give you his number, 01432 760218, and he might be able to sort you out, depending on where you are.

POTATO AND BACK FAT SOUP

To serve six

12 floury potatoes (this is
important as we are aiming at
liquid silk, not wallpaper paste),
peeled and chopped

6 leeks, cleaned and chopped

5 onions, peeled and chopped

10 cloves of garlic, peeled
and chopped

extra virgin olive oil

1 litre light chicken stock

1 litre milk

sea salt and black pepper

TOPPING

125g salted back fat (as with the
wet walnuts, on page 104, but cut
into baked-bean-sized chunks)

OR

6 healthy slices of fresh foie gras

The ultimate soothing yet steadying soup; if feeling a little liverish, or generally frail, this should sort you out.

As with the previous recipe, sweat off all the chopped vegetables and garlic in a pan with the oil. Again I cannot stress enough how much more improved the flavour of the soup will be the longer you can extend this moment. The perfect result would be the potatoes completely cooked (leaving no glimmer of the bitterness of raw potato).

Add the stock and milk and simmer away until all the vegetables have given up any sign of resistance. Put through a fine sieve. Check for seasoning.

Now you have various options; eat the soup as is, which might seem a bit dour. Or, in a frying pan, render your small chunks of salted back fat on not too high a heat, so that you end up with crispy nuduals of salty pork fat to top off the soup. But our possibilities do not end there. You could instead shear off a generous slice of fresh foie gras per bowl of soup, pop on top of the hot soup and give it a few minutes to do a little melting, then eat.

LEEK, POTATO
AND OYSTER SOUP

To serve six

100g butter

9 good leeks, minimally trimmed, keeping all the green, washed and sliced

1 onion, peeled and sliced

5 cloves of garlic, peeled and chopped

4 potatoes, peeled and chopped

1.75 litres light fish or chicken stock

sea salt and black pepper

12 medium rock oysters – it is best you shuck these yourself, as you want to catch every last drop of oyster juice in a bowl

You will need a liquidizer for this recipe, as part of the joy of the dish is the smooth velvety soup within which lurks the oyster.

In a pan large enough to take all the ingredients, melt the butter and sweat your leeks, onion and garlic, avoiding any browning. When these are giving, add the potato and cook amongst the leek mixture for 8 minutes, again avoiding browning. Then add the stock and bring to a gentle boil.

When the potato is cooked, season with salt and pepper. Now liquidize the soup and return it to a clean pan on the heat. Just before eating add the oyster liquor to the soup and place two oysters in each soup bowl. Pour the hot soup over the oysters and eat.

ONION SOUP AND BONE MARROW TOAST

To serve eight

duck fat or butter

2kg onions, peeled, cut in half and sliced

750ml good cider

750ml good veal stock (or if by chance you have some, duck stock)

1 kg middle veal marrowbones

8 slices of white bread

extra virgin olive oil

sea salt and black pepper

a handful of chopped curly parsley

This is the sort of thing Victorians would recommend for a sickly child to make them grow big and strong. It's delicious too.

In a pan large enough to take the other ingredients, melt the duck fat or butter and cook your onions. This time we want them to achieve a soft, sweet brownness (no burning – this is not a process you should rush; it will take up to 1 hour). Once achieved, add the cider and stock, bring to a simmer and cook for 30 minutes. While this is happening, roast your marrowbones in a hot oven until the marrow is loose, not flowing out of the bones. Sprinkle the bread with olive oil and toast in the oven. Season the soup to taste.

When the bones are ready, hold them with a tea towel, scoop out their delicious marrow and spread it on the crispy toast. Sprinkle with coarse sea salt. Serve the soup in deep soup bowls and top with the bone marrow toast. Finish off with a healthy topping of parsley, dropped in the dumper truck style (rather than sprinkled) onto the floating toast. Now eat.

COCK-A-LEEKIE

To serve eight

BRISKET

1kg brined beef brisket (brined as on page 269) for 10–12 days, or salted beef brisket from the butcher

2 onions, peeled

2 carrots, peeled

2 leeks, cleaned

2 bay leaves

10 black peppercorns

a bundle of thyme and parsley

CHICKEN

1 free-range chicken or capon if available (slit the skin where the legs meet the body)

2 peeled onions

2 clean leeks

2 sticks of celery

2 bay leaves

10 black peppercorns

a bundle of thyme

parsley

2 sprigs of rosemary

We made a version of this recently at St. John, and it was so surprising and good that even though it is an old classic I thought I should include this version. I hope that no one will take offence if it seems to break with hundreds of years of cock-a-leekie culture. This is more than a soup, in fact it would happily pass as a meal in itself.

BRISKET

Place the brisket and its accompanying vegetables and herbs in a pan and cover with fresh water. Bring to the boil, then straight away reduce to a very gentle simmer, skimming constantly. This should take about 2½ hours to cook, but always check with a knife how giving the meat is. Allow the beef to cool in the broth.

CHICKEN

Place the chicken in a pan with its team of vegetables and herbs, bring to a boil, then place a lid on the pan and remove from the heat. Allow to cool in the stock. This will make for a moist chicken, as it is to be cooked again.

Remove beef and chicken from their stocks and cut into pieces, not too small but just so it's possible to eat them with a spoon. Strain both stocks, then add the beef stock to the chicken stock to taste. Remember, it will be quite salty, so be cautious – it may not take much. A slight salt undertone is a good thing, though, as it plays very well with the sweet prunes we shall add at the end.

If your combined stock is cloudy or you are anxious about its aesthetic nature, clarify, as on page 267.

FINISHING

5 leeks, cleaned and sliced across

the smallest dash of duck fat or extra virgin olive oil

24 prunes with their stones in (preferably Agen prunes, if you can find them)

FINISHING

Now, in a pan large enough to construct your soup, sweat your sliced leeks in the duck fat or olive oil for about 8 minutes, so as to bring out their sweet leeky nature, but not to lose their crunch. Pour on the stock. Add the chopped chicken and beef, bring to a gentle simmer and let the meat heat through thoroughly. Three minutes before serving add the prunes, just giving them time to puff up.

Serve in big bowls with much bread to hand.

SALADS

(Be firm but fair with salads)

GRILLED JERUSALEM ARTICHOKE, RED ONION AND OLIVES

SNAILS AND OAK LEAF LETTUCE

DECONSTRUCTED PICCALILLI

CUCUMBER, MUSTARD AND DILL

MUSSELS, CUCUMBER AND DILL

PEA AND SHEEP'S MILK CHEESE SALAD

BACON, EGG AND BEAN SALAD

BREAD & WINE SALAD

HOW TO EAT RADISHES AT THEIR PEAK

KOHLRABI

BROAD BEAN AND TROTTER SALAD

WHITE CABBAGE AND BROWN SHRIMP

WARM SALT COD, LITTLE GEM AND TOMATO SALAD

SKATE, CHICORY AND ANCHOVY

ANCHOVY, LITTLE GEM AND TOMATO SALAD

OX TONGUE AND BREAD

BUTTER BEAN, LEEK AND CAULIFLOWER SALAD

BEETROOT, RED ONION, RED CABBAGE, CRÈME FRAÎCHE AND CHERVIL

GRILLED JERUSALEM ARTICHOKE, RED ONION AND OLIVES

To serve four

6 Jerusalem artichokes, washed but not peeled

3 red onions

extra virgin olive oil

a splash of balsamic vinegar

sea salt and black pepper

2 bunches of watercress, woody stalks trimmed off

a handful of small alberquina olives or a firm green olive, e.g. luque royals, so they give a 'gnya' to the salad

a handful of curly parsley, chopped

a splash of Vinaigrette (see page 253)

An autumnal, textural salad.

Boil the artichokes in salted water for 20 minutes until they are giving but not collapsing then allow to cool. Slice lengthwise about 8mm thick and put to one side. Meanwhile skin and quarter the onions, then toss in the olive oil and balsamic vinegar, season with salt and pepper, and roast in a medium to hot oven until soft and sweet. Allow them to cool slightly. Mix the watercress, olives and parsley (parsley acts as a great marrier of disparate parts in a salad, the dating agency of the salad world).

To grill the artichokes, either use a cast-iron ridged griddle or cook them over a barbecue, as it is that nutty seared flavour we are after. They should need no more than 2–3 minutes each side, as long as your griddle or barbecue is hot. Keep an eye on them.

Add them to the other ingredients while warm, then add the vinaigrette, toss and serve.

SNAILS AND OAK LEAF LETTUCE

To serve four

6 shallots, peeled and
finely chopped

8 cloves of garlic, peeled
and finely chopped

a splash of extra virgin olive oil

1 glass of red wine

1 large or 2 small heads of oak leaf
lettuce, washed and separated
but not shredded!

4 pieces of toast (bread sprinkled
with extra virgin olive oil and
baked in the oven until crisp)

sea salt and black pepper

24 snails

a big handful of chopped
curly parsley

a splash of Vinaigrette
(see page 253)

You can pick the snails for this salad yourself. I have done this, though it is quite emotional. A few years ago on Tiree in the Hebrides we collected a positive feast's worth of snails, but what was to follow was too much for one of our party. You have to starve them, so they were put in a bucket covered in pierced cling film to prevent escape and left to purge. Days seemed to pass watching the poor captive snails leaving trails of snail poo on the sides of the bucket. Eventually someone cracked and freed them, much to everyone's relief. If you are of harder heart and can get over this difficult stage, which takes about four days, you should then parboil your snails for about 20 minutes. Remove them from their shells with a pin. Simmer for 1 hour, by which point they will be ready for the salad.

There are English snail farms now, so fresh snails are available (see page 23).

Fry the shallots and garlic in the oil until soft, then add the wine and reduce. While this is happening prepare the base for your salad: put the lettuce into a bowl with the toast slightly broken.

When the wine has reduced so that you have a red moving gunge in your pan, season and toss your snails in the mixture so they are thoroughly heated through. (Alternatively, you can replace them in their shells and smother them with butter, garlic and parsley.) Add the snail mixture to the salad bowl, with the parsley and vinaigrette, toss thoroughly and serve straight away.

DECONSTRUCTED PICCALILLI

To serve six

DRESSING

1 tsp sugar

a splash of red wine vinegar

2 tsp English mustard

*2 cloves of garlic, peeled and
thoroughly crushed*

200ml extra virgin olive oil

sea salt and black pepper

SALAD

*1 cauliflower head, broken into
generous florets*

*1 cucumber, cut into 3 sections,
then sliced in half lengthways,
then each half into 3 long wedges*

*1 red onion, peeled, cut in half and
sliced very thinly*

*600g French beans, topped and
tailed and blanched in boiling
salted water for 3 minutes*

*a handful of capers
(extra-fine if possible)*

A salad created by my sous-chef, Dorothy Harrison. Not too surprisingly, it goes very well with cold meats or oily fish, as well as being a fine dish eaten by itself.

To make the dressing, dissolve the sugar in the red wine vinegar, mix with the other ingredients, and season to taste.

To create the salad simply toss the vegetables and capers in the dressing and serve.

CUCUMBER, MUSTARD AND DILL

Plenty for six people

3 cucumbers, peeled, sliced in half lengthways and seeds removed (a teaspoon is the ideal cucumber gutter)

2 tsp coarse sea salt (Maldon salt is ideal)

a small bunch of dill, picked from the stems

MUSTARD DRESSING
1 tsp white sugar
2 tsp white wine vinegar
1½ tbsp Dijon mustard
extra virgin olive oil
black pepper

This goes very well with such things as cured salmon, mackerel and smoked cod's roe, or is very happily eaten by itself.

I am normally a great believer in slicing things straight across, but the peeled and seeded cucumber is an exception; 8mm slices cut at an angle will give strange wonderful shapes (hopefully).

Place the cucumber in a colander, add the sea salt, and stir it into the cucumber pieces gently with your hands (what we are doing is drawing moisture out of the cucumber, to achieve a crunch with a giving resistance, so one must be careful not to add too much salt because having to rinse the cucumber later will detract from the process). Leave the salted cucumber for 1 hour and in the meantime make the mustard dressing.

Dissolve the sugar (this should not be a sweet dressing, its presence should be subliminal) in the vinegar in a bowl, then spoon in the mustard. Mix thoroughly. Then, gently, mixing all the while, add the olive oil, maintaining an emulsified dressing. Season with black pepper.

Now roughly chop your dill. Shake the excess salty water off the cucumber, and tip the cucumber pieces out onto a clean tea towel. Pat dry. Put the cucumber into a bowl, add the dressing and dill, mix, and serve.

MUSSELS, CUCUMBER AND DILL

To serve four

a splash of extra virgin olive oil

2 onions, peeled and finely chopped

2 sticks of celery, finely chopped

sea salt and black pepper

half a bunch of fresh thyme, tied up

2kg mussels

⅓ bottle of dry white wine

SALAD

1 cucumber

1 red onion, peeled, cut in half
and sliced very thinly

a bunch of dill, picked
from its stems

a small handful of
extra-fine capers

a splash of extra virgin olive oil

juice of 1 lemon

sea salt and black pepper

My first book signing was in a shopping centre in Cambridge. I demonstrated this dish to an audience of two old ladies, one of whom left halfway through. If anyone mentions book signing, images of the shopping centre come back to haunt me. The crunch of the cucumber, the plump orange mussels, the dill and the onions make me happy. The perfect exorcism.

In a lidded pan large enough to fit the mussels, put a splash of oil, heat it up, add the vegetables, and let them fry for a couple of minutes – watch that they do not brown. Season heartily, as you still have the mussels and wine to come, and add the thyme then your mussels and the wine. Stir so they all get to meet the mixture, place the lid on the pan, and cook the mussels, now and then giving the pan a shake. When the mussels open they are cooked. Remove from the heat and allow to cool. When cool pluck the mussels from their shells, and strain and reserve the liquor.

To make the salad, cut the cucumber into 6cm lengths, then split in half, then cut into three lengthwise, aiming the knife blade into the centre of the cucumber. When brought together they should resemble a pile of kindling, rather than cucumber matchsticks. Now mix all the salad ingredients together with the picked mussels and a splash of the reserved mussel liquor, and serve. The orange mussels next to the pale green cucumber flesh is very satisfactory.

PEA AND SHEEP'S MILK CHEESE SALAD

To serve four

200g firm sheep's milk cheese such as Berkswell, grated

100g wafer-thin slices of the same cheese for glamour

2kg young peas in their pods, podded at the last minute

1 spring onion, very finely sliced

a bundle of pea shoots, which are pretty easy to track down now

DRESSING

a splash of sherry vinegar

2 healthy splashes of extra virgin olive oil

sea salt and black pepper

Sweet peas and sharp cheese. This salad rights itself.

With the exception of your glamour slices of cheese, mix all the ingredients in a salad bowl. Add glamour and serve.

BACON, EGG AND BEAN SALAD

thinly sliced yesterday's pot-roast bacon

7-minute boiled eggs, 1½ per person (one of those situations where 1 seems mean, but 2 too much)

green beans, topped and tailed, then cooked in boiling salted water until bendy but not soft

Vinaigrette (see page 253)

lots of chopped curly parsley

Excuse the rather tongue-in-cheek reference to the great national dish.

This is an ideal way to use up leftover pot-roast bacon (see page 132), so it will serve as many as your leftover bacon allows.

Mix all together in a bowl, add bread, wine and friends – the perfect lunch.

BREAD & WINE SALAD
To serve four

5 Little Gem lettuces, cleaned and cut across at 1cm intervals

4 spring onions, finely sliced across

a sprig or two of mint, chopped

juice of ½ lemon

a modest splash of red wine vinegar

a healthy splash of extra virgin olive oil

sea salt and black pepper

The disciplining of vegetables is not to be taken lightly. Letting them know you are in charge is one thing but full-on chopping is another. This salad, created for St. John Bread & Wine, is an example of extreme rigour applied to a Little Gem lettuce.

Mix all together in a bowl. Enjoy the discipline.

HOW TO EAT RADISHES
AT THEIR PEAK

bunches of breakfast radishes (the radish that is like an elongated round with a red top and a white tip) with healthy leaves, gently washed in cold water and shaken dry

coarse sea salt

good unsalted butter

Vinaigrette (see page 253)

The buzzing of the bees, a glass of rosé, the warmth of the sun, radishes and butter.

Pile your intact radishes onto a plate and have beside them a bowl of coarse sea salt and the good butter. To eat, add a knob of butter to your radish with a knife and a sprinkle of salt, then eat. Have a bowl for the discarded leaves and once you have finished the bulbs dress the leaves with as much vinaigrette as seems appropriate and toss then eat this wonderfully peppery salad.

KOHLRABI

I don't think this should be a recipe but more a moment of celebration for this rather unutilized member of the cabbage family, which comes across as more of a root, with a kind of appley turnip quality.

Peeled and sliced thinly, it makes a great addition to a salad – in fact on its own with chervil, capers, lemon and extra virgin olive oil makes for a delicious crunchy salad. Add some finely shaved fennel or chicory – anyway, now I've made the introduction, have fun.

BROAD BEAN AND TROTTER SALAD

To serve four

2kg young broad beans,
podded at the last minute

300g Trotter Gear (see page 130)

4 slices of crunchy toast,
healthily rubbed with raw
garlic, then broken into
quarter-walnut-sized nuggets

a bundle of broad bean shoots and
a handful of finely chopped curly
parsley (if unavailable, wild rocket
or watercress can substitute)

DRESSING

2 healthy splashes of extra virgin
olive oil

a healthy splash of red wine
vinegar

1 tsp Dijon mustard

sea salt and black pepper

Trotters can be summery too.

Pod the broad beans into a bowl. Heat your Trotter Gear. With a holey spoon, scoop the wobbly trotter into the beans. Add the toast, broad bean shoots and chopped parsley or leaves.

Mix together the dressing ingredients. Dress the salad, toss thoroughly and serve.

WHITE CABBAGE
AND BROWN SHRIMP

To serve six

½ standard white cabbage, very thinly sliced – you will be surprised by how much you have once the cabbage is chopped (there is also the gas factor to remember when eating raw cabbage; I think there is only so much the tummy can take)

2 handfuls of peeled brown shrimps (Morecambe Bay)

2 bunches of chervil, 1 chopped finely (for flavour) and the other picked (for the salad's glamour)

DRESSING

juice of 1 lemon

extra virgin olive oil

sea salt and black pepper

This is a wonderful salad.

It is as simple as mixing all the ingredients together so you end up with the little brown shrimps caught in a weave of cabbage. The salty sweetness of the shrimp makes a happy companion to the mysterious warmth of the raw cabbage.

WARM SALT COD, LITTLE GEM AND TOMATO SALAD

To serve four

400g coarse sea salt

450g cod fillet, in one piece, skinned

6 tomatoes

sea salt and black pepper

extra virgin olive oil

2 heads of Little Gem, leaves separated and washed

a healthy spoonful of Aïoli (see page 252)

a handful of chopped curly parsley

This may sound similar to the Anchovy, Little Gem and Tomato Salad overleaf, but it is fundamentally different. We salt our own cod, which has not been dried, so it is firm but has not developed that peculiarly hairy nature which is ideal for other dishes. This is a dish you have to start a week in advance.

A week before you want your salad, find a plastic container in which your cod will fit, also remembering this has to sit in your fridge for 6 days. Line the base of the container with a layer of sea salt, lay the cod fillet on top, then cover this with more sea salt. Cover with cling film or a lid and place in the fridge.

On the sixth day remove the cod from the salt and rinse under gentle running water, then soak in clean water for 12 hours, changing it regularly.

Slice the tomatoes in half lengthwise, sprinkle with salt and pepper and oil and roast in a medium oven for approximately 20 minutes. This will soften and slightly dry them, intensifying and sweetening their flavour. Allow to cool, and reserve the cooking juices.

Place the Little Gem leaves and tomato halves into a bowl and mix the remaining oily roast-tomato juice with the spoonful of aïoli for your dressing.

When all is ready, bring a pan of fresh water up to a gentle simmer. Chop your cod into 2.5cm cubes and poach them in your simmering water for 5 minutes. If they fall apart slightly, do not worry, they will still taste delicious. Gently remove with a slotted spoon, shake off the water and add to the other ingredients waiting in the bowl. Dress with your tomato/aïoli dressing and add the handful of parsley. Carefully but thoroughly toss the salad and eat.

SKATE, CHICORY AND ANCHOVY

To serve six

1 skate wing, approximately
600–800g – get your fishmonger
to skin it for you, both sides

POACHING BROTH

enough water to cover your skate

1 glass of white wine

zest of 1 lemon

1 head of fennel, sliced

1 onion, peeled and sliced

2 sticks of celery, chopped

1 whole garlic, chopped in half

whole black peppercorns

a bunch of parsley, tied

sea salt

ANCHOVY DRESSING

20 anchovy fillets

8 cloves of garlic, peeled

a healthy splash of red wine
vinegar

150ml extra virgin olive oil

black pepper

SALAD

2 heads of green chicory, or 3 of
white, chopped

a bunch of rocket, picked

a handful of chopped curly parsley

a small handful of capers
(extra-fine if possible)

When poached and allowed to grow cold, skate sets beautifully into a firm but giving fish whose natural structure shreds perfectly for our salad-making purposes.

To make your poaching broth mix all the ingredients together. Bring it up to the boil and then turn the heat down to a simmer.

Slip your skate wing into the poaching pan and cook for approximately 10 minutes (check that the flesh comes away from the bone), then turn off the heat and allow to cool in the liquor.

When cold remove the skate from the liquor and pull the flesh from the bone. It should come away in easy strips.

Now make your dressing: either whizz all the ingredients in a food processor or pound them in a mortar with a pestle.

Bring together the skate, the salad ingredients and the anchovy dressing (caution – there may be too much, so do not add it all at once) and toss.

ANCHOVY, LITTLE GEM AND TOMATO SALAD

To serve four

6 tomatoes, the happiest you can find (it is possible to find tomatoes on the vine)

sea salt and black pepper

extra virgin olive oil

a handful of chopped curly parsley

16 good anchovy fillets in oil, separated but kept whole

2 heads of Little Gem lettuce, washed and separated, not shredded

a splash of Vinaigrette (see page 253)

Amazingly uplifting powers for a simple salad.

Slice the tomatoes in half lengthwise, sprinkle with salt and pepper and oil, and roast in a medium oven for approximately 20 minutes. This will soften and slightly dry them, intensifying and sweetening their flavour. Allow to cool.

Mix all the ingredients in a bowl and eat.

OX TONGUE AND BREAD

To serve four

16 x 1.5cm cubes of yesterday's
white bread with crust removed

a healthy dollop of Green Sauce
(see page 255)

16 thin slices of cold boiled
salted ox tongue, like little
angels' wings (one tongue
will supply this and more)

8 trimmed spring onions

2 bunches of rocket (wild if possible),
trimmed (this can be replaced by
watercress)

a bunch of sorrel, picked
from the stems

8 young borage leaves, if you
can get them

a splash of Vinaigrette
(see page 253) or extra
virgin olive oil and
lemon juice

Cold tongue, need I say more.

Place the bread cubes in your salad bowl with the Green Sauce,
so they have a chance to absorb some of it. Then gently toss the rest
of the ingredients into the bowl, trying to keep the slices of tongue
reasonably intact. If it seems a wee bit dry, loosen with an extra
splash of vinaigrette or oil and lemon juice.

BUTTER BEAN, LEEK AND CAULIFLOWER SALAD

To serve four to six

2 handfuls of butter beans

2 heads of garlic

1 happy head of cauliflower, taken apart into challenging bite-sized florets

4 leeks, sliced across at 5mm intervals, then thoroughly rinsed

a bunch of curly parsley, finely chopped

a handful of extra-fine capers

DRESSING

300ml extra virgin olive oil – it's a thirsty salad

juice of 1 juicy or 2 not so juicy lemons

6 cloves of garlic, peeled and thoroughly crushed (this may seem a lot, but remember the dressing has to bring 'wayhey' to some very calm elements)

sea salt and black pepper

Unusually for a salad, this enjoys sitting, getting to know its dressing. It is inspired by Ellen Hooberman, a master of the caper, garlic and chopped parsley, which is a good thing!

Soak the butter beans overnight in cold water, then drain and cook in clean water with the heads of garlic (this can take 2–3 hours) so that you have your aforementioned pillows of joy (see page 20).

Whisk all the dressing ingredients together thoroughly, adding salt and pepper to taste.

Take the cauliflower and butter beans and liberally dress them. Toss and then leave to sit overnight.

When it comes time to serve, just tease the leeks for a moment in some boiling salted water. The warmth of the leek, added to the cauliflower and butter beans, should awaken the slumbering salad. Once awake, it may need some more dressing – take a view. Add the chopped parsley and a substantial handful of capers. Toss vigorously, being careful not to crush the butter beans, then serve.

BEETROOT, RED ONION, RED CABBAGE, CRÈME FRAÎCHE AND CHERVIL

To serve six

2 raw beetroot, peeled and finely grated

¼ raw red cabbage with its core cut out, very finely sliced

1 small red onion, peeled, cut in half from top to bottom and finely sliced

6 healthy dollops of crème fraîche

2 healthy bunches of chervil, picked from the stems

DRESSING

healthy splashes of extra virgin olive oil

a little gesture of balsamic vinegar

a small handful of extra-fine capers

sea salt and black pepper

Too often you are offered a *fait accompli* on a plate, a weave of ingredients in which your only involvement will be to make a mess of it, with the inevitable intervention of your knife and fork. Well, here is a salad that welcomes the messing-up process.

Mix everything together for the dressing. Toss all your raw red vegetables in the dressing, then on six plates place a bushel of this red mixture. Next to this, nustle your blob of crème fraîche as if the two ingredients were good friends, not on top of each other as if they were lovers. Finally, rest a clump of the chervil next to the other ingredients in the friendly fashion.

A very striking salad ready for the eater to mess up.

SMALLER BUT OFTEN SUSTAINING DISHES

ROAST BONE MARROW AND PARSLEY SALAD
CURED BEEF AND CELERIAC
JELLIED TRIPE
CALF'S BRAIN TERRINE
CALVES' BRAINS, CHICORY AND SHALLOTS
COLD CALVES' BRAINS ON TOAST
DEEP-FRIED CALVES' BRAINS
GRILLED, MARINATED CALF'S HEART
COLD ROAST BEEF ON DRIPPING TOAST
DUCKS' HEARTS ON TOAST
DUCK'S NECK TERRINE
PICKLED HERRINGS
CELERY SALT AND BOILED EGGS

ROAST BONE MARROW AND PARSLEY SALAD

To serve four

12 x 7–8cm pieces of middle veal marrowbone

a healthy bunch of flat parsley, picked from its stems

2 shallots, peeled and very thinly sliced

1 modest handful of capers (extra-fine if possible)

DRESSING

juice of 1 lemon

extra virgin olive oil

a pinch of sea salt and black pepper

a good supply of toast

This is the one dish that does not change on the menu at St. John. The marrowbone comes from a calf's leg; ask your butcher to keep some for you. You will need teaspoons or long thin implements to scrape your marrow out of the bone.

Do you recall eating Sultana Bran for breakfast? The sultana to bran-flake ratio was always a huge anxiety, to a point, sometimes, that one was tempted to add extra sultanas, which inevitably resulted in too many sultanas, and one lost that pleasure of discovering the occasional sweet chewiness in contrast to the branny crunch. With administering such things as capers it is very good to remember Sultana Bran.

Put the bone marrow in an ovenproof frying pan and place in a hot oven. The roasting process should take about 20 minutes depending on the thickness of the bone. You are looking for the marrow to be loose and giving, but not melted away, which it will do if left too long (traditionally the ends would be covered to prevent any seepage, but I like the colouring and crispness at the end).

Meanwhile lightly chop your parsley, just enough to discipline it, mix it with the shallots and capers, and at the last moment, dress.

Here is a dish that should not be completely seasoned before leaving the kitchen, rendering seasoning by the actual eater unnecessary; a last-minute seasoning, especially in the case of coarse sea salt, gives texture and uplift at the moment of eating. My approach is to scrape the marrow from the bone onto the toast and season with coarse sea salt. Then a pinch of parsley salad on top of this and eat. Of course once you have your pile of bones, salad, toast and salt it is Liberty Hall.

CURED BEEF
AND CELERIAC

To serve twelve

400g coarse sea salt

600g sugar

10 sprigs of rosemary

*1 fillet of beef
(ask your butcher to trim it)*

*a handful of finely cracked
black pepper*

1 head of celeriac, peeled

juice of 1 lemon

1½ tbsp Dijon mustard

4 tbsp crème fraîche

sea salt and black pepper

This curing process can also be used on a fillet of venison.

Mix the salt and sugar together. Take a plastic container into which your fillet will fit uncured and which will fit in your fridge, and place 5 sprigs of rosemary in the bottom. Generously cover with the salt and sugar mix, lay the fillet onto this, then cover with the rest of the mix (if you have not got enough of the salt and sugar mixture, simply make up some more, 40 per cent salt to 60 per cent sugar). Nestle the rest of the rosemary into this. Cover the container and refrigerate for 3 days.

Remove the fillet from the now damp salt and sugar, rinse under cold running water, and dry with a clean cloth. When dry, take a handful of cracked pepper and rub the firm fillet all over; this should remove any remaining moisture and give an *oomph* to the meat. Wrap in cling film and keep in the fridge until you use it (this is not a long curing process and as a result the meat will not keep for more than a week and should be refrigerated).

Slice the celeriac very thinly, using the width of a match as a rough guide, then lay a manageable pile of slices flat and slice again into match widths. At this point a mandolin is very useful, but if you don't have one, do not fear, you can easily achieve matchstick strips of celeriac with a knife. As you go squeeze lemon juice over your growing mound of celeriac strands to prevent them going brown when finished. Fold the Dijon mustard and crème fraîche gently together – don't beat, as the cream will lose its structure. Season to taste and mix this through the celeriac.

To serve the beef, slice thinly across. You will have beautiful dark red flesh – the colour of a fine old master comes to mind. The spirited white celeriac makes a splendid accompaniment.

If you don't eat it that day, it will be fine the next if kept in the fridge.

JELLIED TRIPE

To serve four

4 pig's trotters

2 whole heads of garlic

bay leaves

a bundle of thyme

2 litres good dry cider

1 glass of Calvados (optional)

2kg tripe

a scoop of duck fat

8 shallots, peeled and finely sliced

4 carrots, peeled and finely sliced

2 leeks, cleaned, peeled and finely sliced

6 cloves of garlic, peeled and finely chopped

4 tinned plum tomatoes

sea salt and black pepper

This is summer captured in jelly.

Place the trotters, whole heads of garlic, bay leaves, thyme, cider and Calvados, if using, in a pot. Bring up to the boil, and reduce to a simmer. After 2 hours add the tripe. Cook for approximately another 1–1½ hours, until the tripe and trotters are cooked: when you pinch them, your fingers easily go through the flesh. Remove the tripe, trotters, herbs and garlic from the liquor, which you should leave cooking to reduce by half. Pull the flesh off the trotters while still warm and add to the tripe, discarding the bones.

Meanwhile sweat in the duck fat the shallots, carrots, leeks and chopped garlic until softened, but not a pulp. Add the tomatoes, crushing them in your hand as you do so, and let this mixture cook for a further 20 minutes, sweetening the tomatoes (you are not looking to make a tomato dish, just bring the faintest blush). Now add the tripe and trotter flesh to the pot with a few ladles of the liquor, and season to taste. Remember that this will be served cold, so slightly overcompensate. Let this cook gently together for another 30 minutes.

Line a terrine mould or bread tin with cling film. Spoon in the tripe, trotter and vegetables with a slotted spoon, topping up at the end with liquid so they're just covered. Make sure, by banging the mould on the table, you are not left with any gaps or air holes. Cover with cling film and leave in the fridge overnight to set.

When firm, remove it from the fridge to acclimatize without getting too warm, and slice it as you would a terrine: you should have a beautiful cross-section through a tripey weave. Serve with chicory salad dressed with Dijon mustard, red wine vinegar, extra virgin olive oil, capers and parsley.

CALF'S BRAIN TERRINE

Plenty for ten to twelve people

8 calves' brains, rinsed thoroughly in cold water

2 cloves of garlic, peeled and chopped

2 shallots, peeled and chopped

2 duck livers

300g lean pork, chopped

300g lean veal, chopped

300g pork back fat, chopped into chunks

a healthy pinch of ground black pepper

a healthy pinch of ground allspice

a small pinch of ground cinnamon

a small pinch of ground clove

a small pinch of ground nutmeg

a splash of brandy

600g good green streaky bacon, thinly sliced (enough to line your terrine mould or bread tin and cover the top)

sea salt (but be cautious, because your bacon and your back fat may have been salted – if this is so do not add salt)

This recipe is closely inspired by a recipe of Paula Wolfert's who, in turn, points out she has been inspired by Lucien Vanel; so thank you, Lucien Vanel, and indeed Paula Wolfert.

As well as being delicious and textural to eat, this terrine, when sliced, beautifully exposes a cross-section of a brain, caught in a meaty square. Although this may not sound it to all, it is a thing of beauty.

In gently boiling water blanch your brains for 4 minutes then carefully remove them with a slotted spoon. Refresh them in ice-cold water, and drain on a clean tea towel.

In a food processor (or by hand, chopping the ingredients very finely) whizz the garlic first until it is a purée, then add the shallots and the duck livers so that they merge with the garlic purée, followed by the pork, veal and back fat. Caution, you do not want this mixture too fine! Keep your finger near the off button. Texture is a grand thing in a terrine. Tip this into a mixing bowl and season with the spices and the splash of brandy. Mix. (Allspice, cinnamon, clove and nutmeg are known as *quatre épices*, vital in most terrine and sausage making, as ground meat often loses its flavour and needs these spices' help to find it again.)

Line your terrine mould or bread tin with the streaky bacon, leaving flaps to cover the top of the terrine. Fill the terrine mould up to a third of the way up with the terrine mix, then run the brains down the middle all the way along, nestling them close together so everyone will have a good, brainy slice. Cover with the rest of the mix, then bring your bacon flaps over to cover the top of the terrine and cover with tinfoil.

Fold a tea towel in half and lay it in a deep roasting tray (this will calm the direct heat on the bottom of the terrine), place the terrine mould on top of this and surround with enough water to come two-thirds of the way up the mould's side, and place in a medium hot oven for 2 hours. Check that the centre of the terrine is hot with a skewer and remove from the oven and its watery tray. Allow to rest for a few minutes, then remove the foil and replace it with new foil. Put the terrine under pressure with some weights and, in this condition, once cooled let it sit in the fridge for 2 days then eat.

CALVES' BRAINS, CHICORY AND SHALLOTS

To serve four

4 heads of chicory

5 knobs of butter

juice of 1 lemon

sea salt and black pepper

12 shallots, peeled but kept whole

oil

6 calves' brains, rinsed and blanched as for frying (see overleaf), lobes separated

a splash of chicken stock

a splash of sherry vinegar

a handful of capers (extra-fine if possible)

a handful of chopped curly parsley

You don't want your pan to be too hot. You're not looking for a singe, more of a nutty crust.

Place the chicory heads in an ovenproof dish just big enough to fit them, apply 4 of the knobs of butter, pour over the lemon juice, and season. Cover with tinfoil and put into a medium to hot oven for 40 minutes. Remove from the oven and allow to cool. Leave the oven on.

Place the shallots in an ovenproof frying pan, toss with oil, and season. Put into the oven at the same temperature and roast until soft, sweet and giving (approximately 20 minutes). Now get a large frying pan hot, then reduce the heat, add the remaining knob of butter, and when melted and sizzling, add the brains. Brown gently on both sides. It is important not to be too ferocious doing this, to get a reasonably even golden crispiness on your brains. Remove the brains and keep warm.

Slice the chicory in half lengthwise and place in the frying pan. Gently colour and heat through on both sides. Add the shallots, brains and chicken stock, and season. Raise the heat slightly and let all the ingredients get to know each other. Just before serving, add the sherry vinegar and let this sizzle for a moment, then place on a hot plate. To serve, scatter with a subliminal showing of capers, and then parsley. Eat while hot, making sure you have some crusty white bread to hand for supping up the juices.

COLD CALVES' BRAINS ON TOAST

To serve four

2 onions, peeled

2 carrots, peeled

2 leeks, peeled

2 sticks of celery

1 whole head of garlic

black peppercorns in muslin

bay leaf

a bundle of fresh herbs

4 calves' brains, rinsed
in cold water

4 pieces of bread, long
rather than square

a splash of extra virgin olive oil

Green Sauce (see page 255)

sea salt

This is a dish for those who particularly enjoy the texture of brain.

Bring a pan of water with all the stock vegetables and herbs up to a simmer for 15 minutes. Then *gently* lower your calves' brains into the pot, let them cook gently for 8 minutes, remove with a slotted spoon, and leave to cool on a tray. Meanwhile toast the bread.

When the brains are cold and firm, separate the lobes, slice lengthwise 6mm thick, lay in fish-scale fashion on the toast, lightly dressed with olive oil. Top with some Green Sauce (the give of the brains, then the crunch of the toast, and the bite of the sauce).

DEEP-FRIED CALVES' BRAINS
To feed four

2 onions, peeled

2 carrots, peeled

2 leeks, peeled

2 sticks of celery

1 whole head of garlic

black peppercorns in muslin

bay leaf

a bundle of fresh herbs

6 calves' brains,
rinsed in cold water

plain flour, seasoned with
sea salt and black pepper

4 eggs

250ml milk

fine dry white breadcrumbs

vegetable oil for deep frying

Green Sauce (see page 255)

A crispy cloud of joy.

Bring a pan of water with all the stock vegetables and herbs up to a simmer for 15 minutes. Then *gently* lower your calves' brains into the pot, let them cook gently for 6 minutes, remove with a slotted spoon, and leave to cool on a tray. When the brains are cold and firm, separate the lobes.

Meanwhile prepare three bowls: the first with the seasoned plain flour in; the second with the eggs and milk whisked together; the third with the breadcrumbs.

Heat up your oil for deep frying: once you have coated the brains, you don't want to leave the crusts to get soggy.

It is a great help to have an extra pair of hands at this point for the tossing and rolling, but if they're not available, try to keep one hand dry and one eggy, otherwise you start to form great lumps of flour, egg and bread on your hands, which will transfer to the brains.

Roll a brain in flour, then coat it in the egg mix and finish with a roll in the breadcrumbs. With a small shake carefully set it aside for frying.

When the oil is hot pop the brains in until crisp: this will take a matter of minutes. Drain on kitchen paper and serve hot with Green Sauce. The result is like biting through crunch into a rich cloud.

GRILLED, MARINATED CALF'S HEART

To serve four

1 calf's heart

a healthy splash of balsamic vinegar

coarse sea salt

black pepper

chopped fresh thyme

This is a wonderfully simple, delicious dish, the heart not, as you might imagine, tough as old boots due to all the work it does, but in fact firm and meaty but giving.

Trim the heart of anything that looks like sinew (this is easy enough to spot) and excess fat (which tends to be around the open top of the heart), and remove any blood clots lurking in the ventricles. Slice the heart open so you can lay it flat and complete the process. Then cut it into pieces approximately 2–3cm square, up to 5mm thick; if the flesh suddenly gets thick, simply slice it in half horizontally through the meat.

Toss the pieces of heart in the balsamic vinegar, salt, pepper and thyme. Leave to marinate for 24 hours.

Now for cooking you need a cast-iron griddle or a barbecue. Get it very hot and apply the heart: it will take about 3 minutes each side. Serve with a spirited salad of your choice, e.g. watercress, shallot and bean, or raw leek.

COLD ROAST BEEF ON DRIPPING TOAST

One of those treats for the day after, having saved the dripping from the previous day's roast.

Spread dripping onto a slice of white toast and put under the grill for a moment to make sure it melts completely. Sprinkle with coarse sea salt and pop a thin slice of yesterday's cold beef on top. Open a jar of pickled walnuts. A glass of something Burgundian. Life is good!

DUCKS' HEARTS ON TOAST

To serve one

a knob of butter

5 ducks' hearts (in an ideal world, otherwise as many as you can muster up)

a splash of balsamic vinegar

a splash of chicken stock

sea salt and black pepper

1 slice of toast

The perfect snack for the cook who has just prepared 5 ducks.

Have your toast ready.

Get a frying pan very hot, pop in your knob of butter, followed by the hearts, and fry them for 4 minutes, rolling them around occasionally. Apply a splash of balsamic vinegar and chicken stock, season, and let the hearts get to know the liquor for a couple of minutes. Place the hearts on the toast, leave the sauce on the heat to reduce for a moment, and pour over the toast and duck hearts. Eat. The hearts have an amazingly ducky quality.

DUCK'S NECK TERRINE

To serve four

8 ducks' necks, skins removed and reserved

12 ducks' gizzards, cleaned and trimmed

3 ducks' legs

350g pork belly, diced

coarse sea salt

half a bunch of fresh thyme

duck fat – a large tin should suffice

100g smoked streaky bacon, finely cubed

allspice, crushed

mace, crushed

cracked black pepper

400g back fat (very thinly sliced)

225g prunes, soaked in hot tea with a healthy splash of brandy in it for at least 24 hours

If you find yourself with a few duck necks, this is a splendid dish.

Place the skinned ducks' necks, gizzards, and legs with the pork belly in a plastic or china container, sprinkle with salt and thyme sprigs, toss so the salt gets all around, cover, and leave in the fridge for 24 hours. Shake off the salt and thyme, lay in an oven tray, and cover with duck fat. Cover with tinfoil and place in a medium oven until the flesh is giving and just coming away from the bone (approximately 2–2½ hours).

Tip into a container to cool. You should keep confit for months to develop, but in this case you are allowed to speed things along. Remove the legs and necks from the fat and pull the meat away from the bones. In a bowl mix this with the pork belly, gizzards, bacon and enough duck fat to keep it a moving mixture and season with allspice, mace and pepper (salt is unnecessary due to the bacon). Remember this will be served cold, so compensate with generous seasoning.

Meanwhile, roll out a piece of cling film on which you lay a regimented row of thinly sliced back fat as long as your terrine mould or bread tin. Lay a lengthways row of your soaked prunes two-thirds of the way up the row. Then, using the cling film to lift the fat, fold the top third back over the prunes, press down, and remove the cling film. Then, again using the cling film, bring the other two-thirds of fat over the almost covered prunes, then gently roll the whole thing back towards you, at which point you should have a perfect prune/fat roll. Remove the cling film.

Line your terrine mould with the duck's neck skin as you would with bacon, leaving flaps hanging over the side to cover the top. Fill the lined mould a third of the way up with the duck and pork mixture, then lay your prune roll down the middle. Cover with more mixture up to just below the top of the mould, flip over the duck's neck flaps, and top off with foil.

Line the bottom of a deep oven tray with a tea towel folded in half (this diffuses the direct heat from the base of the tray), sit your terrine and mould on the towel, and surround with water. Follow the height of the oven tray and terrine mould: don't go over either edge and allow enough leeway for waves as you move the tray. Put into a medium oven for 2 hours.

Remove the tray from the oven and the terrine from the tray. Replace the tinfoil with new foil, cut a piece of card to match the opening of your terrine mould, place this on top, and apply weights to press the terrine. Allow to cool and put it in the fridge for 24 hours to allow it to find itself.

To serve, take it from the fridge to acclimatize, then remove it from the mould and slice: you should have something resembling a terrazzo floor with a prune eye in the middle. Serve with bread, cornichons and red wine.

PICKLED HERRINGS

To serve two to four

8 herrings

200g coarse sea salt

550g sugar

450ml white wine vinegar

300ml water

14 whole allspice

14 black peppercorns

2 carrots, peeled and thinly sliced

3 red onions, peeled
and thinly sliced

4cm piece of fresh horseradish,
peeled and thinly sliced

3 bay leaves

Two pickled herring fillets will do handsomely as a starter and three will happily pass as a light lunch. Eat with their pickled vegetables, a blob of crème fraîche and capers. Or, allowing two fillets per person, chop the pickled herring fillets across into 2cm sections, mix with hot sliced boiled potatoes, the pickled vegetables and capers, dress with extra virgin olive oil, toss and serve while the potatoes are still warm.

To fillet the herrings, lay them flat on one side and with a thin, sharp knife cut just behind the gills until you feel the blade touch the backbone, then turn the blade towards the tail; hold the head and slip the knife tailwards along the backbone. Turn the fish over and repeat the process. You may have to trim off some of the remaining herring ribs. (Or ask your fishmonger.)

Mix the salt and 300g of the sugar together, and place your herring fillets in a plastic container, sprinkling this mixture between each layer. Leave in the fridge for 24 hours. This will lead to a firmer, more flavoursome final result. Next day rinse off the sugar and salt and drain the herrings.

In a stainless-steel pan, heat up the vinegar, water and remaining sugar, until the sugar is thoroughly dissolved. Remove from the heat and allow to cool. In the container in which you intend to store your pickled herrings (plastic, glass or china), layer the fillets with your spices, sliced vegetables and bay leaves equally spread about, then cover with the cooled sugar solution. Leave for a week before eating; they will keep very well in the fridge.

CELERY SALT
AND BOILED EGGS

400g coarse sea salt

400g grated peeled celeriac

free-range eggs

This is where it all started.

Mix the salt and celeriac, put into a plastic container, and cover. Leave in the fridge for 2 days, allowing time for the celeriac and salt to get to know each other. Then lay out the mixture in an oven tray and bake in a gentle oven for about 2–3 hours until thoroughly dried out and crisp; check frequently to avoid any singeing as this will give the celery salt a burnt taste. Crush the dried salt and celeriac in a food processor or use a mortar and pestle. The celery salt will keep for ages in an airtight container.

Cook your eggs in gently boiling water for 8 minutes, then cool under running cold water, which should result in a slightly yielding yolk.

Serve together. Peel your egg, dip it in the salt, and eat.

CHEESY MOMENTS

WELSH RAREBIT
WIGMORE AND POTATO PIE
FENNEL AND BERKSWELL

WELSH RAREBIT

Makes four pieces

a knob of butter

1 tbsp flour

1 tsp English mustard powder

½ tsp cayenne pepper

200ml Guinness

a very long splash of
Worcestershire sauce

450g mature strong
Cheddar cheese, grated

4 pieces of toast

We all love cheesy toast!

Melt the butter in a pan, stir in the flour, and let the mixture cook until
it smells biscuity but is not browning. Add the mustard powder and
cayenne pepper then stir in the Guinness and Worcestershire sauce,
then gently melt in the cheese. When it's all of one consistency remove
from the heat, pour out into a shallow container, and allow to set.

Spread on toast 1cm thick and place under the grill. Eat when bubbling
golden brown. This makes a splendid savoury at the end of your meal,
washed down with a glass of port, or a steadying snack.

WIGMORE AND POTATO PIE

To serve two

4 potatoes,
boiled and peeled

1 ripe Wigmore cheese

sea salt and black pepper

1 egg, lightly beaten

DOUGH

420g plain flour, sifted

2 eggs

1 egg yolk

100g warm melted butter

a pinch of salt

100ml warm water

When you turn the pie out of the tin it resembles a cottage with subsidence. Word of warning: you want everyone at the table before you put your knife into the pie.

Don't let the dough go cold or it will be difficult to use. The quantity given here makes enough for two goes, just in case.

To make the dough, place the flour, eggs, egg yolk, melted butter and salt in the bowl of an electric mixer. Using the beater attachment, mix the ingredients to a firm paste. Add the water and mix again until a soft, glossy, pliable dough is formed. Cover the bowl with a cloth and leave in a warm place for 30 minutes.

While the dough is resting, cut the potatoes into slices 1cm thick and do the same with the Wigmore cheese. Grease a 16 x 10 x 8cm loaf tin with butter and then dust it with flour.

Roll out half the pastry very thinly – about 3mm thick. Try to do this quite quickly so it doesn't go cold. Use the rolled-out dough to line the loaf tin, making sure you have about 2cm overhanging; trim off the rest. Cover the base of the pastry with some of the sliced potatoes – you will have to trim them a little – then season with salt and pepper. Add a layer of Wigmore cheese. Carry on layering until you reach the top of the tin, ending with a layer of potatoes.

Roll out a lid for the pie from the dough trimmings. Place the lid on top of the potatoes, then brush the overhanging dough with the beaten egg and fold it over the pastry lid to seal. Brush the top with more egg.

Place in an oven preheated to 180°C/Gas Mark 4 and bake for about 1 hour, until golden brown on top and piping hot in the middle. Serve with pickled walnuts.

FENNEL AND BERKSWELL

Berkswell, for those of you who have not encountered it before, is a magnificent, firm sheep's milk cheese. It seems almost cheeky to be cooking with it, but the results are splendid.

In an ovenproof dish, layer up fennel, sliced against the grain, and grated Berkswell, ending with a Berkswell layer. Season the dish, splash with milk so everything is more damp than wet, then cover and put into a gentle oven. Let it calmly do its thing.

After 2½ hours, take the lid off for a bit of colour. What you should end up with is a cake of sweet, collapsing fennel and curds and whey, like cheesy nuduals. As a dish, it has no end of companions, but will also stand alone with just a pickled walnut to keep it company.

THE PIG

PORK SCRATCHINGS, A VERSION OF
CONFIT PIG'S CHEEK AND DANDELION
PIG'S CHEEK AND TONGUE
BRAWN
SORREL, CHICORY AND CRISPY EAR SALAD
PRESSED PIG'S EAR
BATH CHAPS
PIG'S HEAD AND POTATO PIE
PIG'S HEAD AND BEANS
WARM PIG'S HEAD
POT-ROAST HALF PIG'S HEAD
PIG'S TROTTER STUFFED WITH POTATO
SALTED BACK FAT AND WET WALNUTS
DRIED SALTED PIG'S LIVER, RADISHES AND BOILED EGGS
ROLLED PIG'S SPLEEN
ROAST PORK LOIN, TURNIPS, GARLIC AND ANCHOVIES
BEANS AND BACON
BACON KNUCKLE AND PICKLED CABBAGE
BOILED BELLY AND LENTILS
BRINED PORK BELLY, ROASTED
BOILED HAM AND PARSLEY SAUCE
BROAD BEANS, HAM AND PARSLEY SAUCE
HAM IN HAY
CURED HAM
CRISPY PIGS' TAILS
BLOOD CAKE AND FRIED EGGS
ROAST WHOLE SUCKLING PIG

PORK SCRATCHINGS, A VERSION OF

sea salt

pig's skin (ask your butcher), with some fat attached

enough duck fat to cover the skin

A most steadying nibble.

Spread a layer of sea salt on a plastic tray, or anything that won't react with the salt. Lay the skin on top and sprinkle liberally with sea salt. Leave in the fridge for 5 days.

When its time is up, remove the skin from the fridge and soak overnight in cold water. Rinse in clean water. Thoroughly dry with a clean tea towel and lay it in an oven tray. Cover with duck fat, then cover the tray with foil. Cook in a medium oven for 2½ hours. As with all things cooking, keep an eye on it.

Take it out of the oven and allow to cool, smearing it with the solidifying duck fat. At this point you can keep it in the fridge until your next drinks party, or a frail moment when you are in need of such nourishment.

When such a moment arrives, place a rack on an oven tray, then lay your skin on top. Again put into a medium oven, in which it should slightly puff up into a sheet of golden, crispy joy (be careful not to brown it, as this is bitter and sad). Now remove from the oven and allow to cool. Place the crispy skin on a board and chop it with a heavy knife. It should break up into pieces. Serve.

A word of warning, though: with fragile dental arrangements, eat with caution.

CONFIT PIG'S CHEEK AND DANDELION

To serve four

a handful of coarse sea salt

4 pig's cheeks

duck or goose fat

12 shallots, peeled and left whole

12 cloves of garlic, peeled and left whole

4 slices of good bread

a bunch of dandelion leaves

a handful of extra-fine capers

a bunch of parsley, finely chopped

Vinaigrette (see page 253)

A dish that could be accused of being a salad, but I see it more as lunch.

Ask your butcher for pigs' cheeks; you need the skin and fat on, not just the nuggets of flesh. This should not be too difficult, given a day or two's warning.

Salt your cheeks and leave overnight. Next day, brush them off thoroughly with a clean kitchen cloth, then lay them in a deepish oven dish and cover with duck or goose fat. Cover with foil and pop them into a gentle to medium oven for approximately 3 hours. Keep an eye on them; you want a giving cheek when stabbed with a sharp knife. When happy with the stabbing, remove them from the oven and allow to cool in the fat. At this point you could keep the cheeks covered in the fat in the fridge for a rainy day or proceed by removing them from the fat. Scrape off any excess with your fingers and keep the fat for future use.

Don't forget your shallots and garlic. Put them in an ovenproof dish, cover with duck or goose fat and roast until soft, sweet and giving.

Place the slices of bread in an ovenproof dish, on top of which you should rest your cheeks. Slip it into a medium oven and allow the cheeks to loosen up, the fat to crisp up and the bread to absorb all the goodness – about 1½ hours.

When the cheeks are crispy, you are ready. Place the dandelion leaves in a bowl with the shallots, garlic, capers and parsley. Then lay your bread and cheeks on a board and chop into spirited chunks with a heavy knife. Add them to your leaves of dandelion. Dress. Toss with conviction, open the red wine and away you go …

PIG'S CHEEK AND TONGUE
To feed two

a brine (see page 269)

1 pig's head

stock vegetables – carrots, leeks, onion, celery

a bundle of fresh herbs

black peppercorns

a splash of red wine vinegar

Tongue-in-cheek.

Brine your pig's head for 3 days, rinse it, and place it in a large pot with the stock vegetables, herbs, peppercorns and vinegar. Cover with water and bring to the boil. Reduce to a gentle simmer and cook for 2½–3 hours. The cheeks should come away easily from the skull; keep these warm in the broth.

Open the pig's jaw and pull out the tongue. Peel it while still warm and slice in half lengthways, so each diner gets a cheek and half a tongue. Serve with mashed potato and Green Sauce (see page 255).

BRAWN

To serve eight

1 pig's head, rinsed thoroughly

4 pig's trotters

2 onions, peeled

2 carrots, peeled

2 leeks, cleaned

2 sticks of celery

2 whole heads of garlic

zest of 2 lemons

a healthy splash of
red wine vinegar

a bundle of fresh herbs

2 bay leaves

a scant handful of black
peppercorns (tied up in
muslin or you will be
picking them out of the
cooked meat for ever)

sea salt

You can use the pig's ears to make the Sorrel, Chicory and Crispy Ear Salad (see opposite), which is an ideal accompaniment. If not, remove them before you start to make the brawn.

Place the head and trotters into a large pot, cover with water, and add all the other ingredients except salt. As soon as you have brought it up to the boil, reduce to a very gentle simmer, skimming as you go.

If using, extract the ears after about 1 hour, rinse them and dry them carefully. When you can feel the cheek starting to come away from the bone (this should take about 2½ hours), remove everything from the liquor and discard the vegetables. Return the liquor to the heat to reduce by about half, then season with salt, remembering this is served cold, which subdues flavours. While still warm, pick through the trotters and pig's head retrieving the flesh, especially peeling the tongue. The snout is neither fat nor meat; do not be discouraged, it is delicious in your brawn.

Line your terrine mould with cling film and fill with the retrieved meats. Cover with enough of the reduced liquor just to cover, slamming the mould on the kitchen table to shake out any air bubbles. Leave to set overnight in the fridge, and before serving, remove it in good time to acclimatize without being so warm it is soft and sweaty. Serve with a sorrel, chicory and crispy ear salad.

SORREL, CHICORY AND CRISPY EAR SALAD

To serve eight

2 boiled pig's ears (see opposite)

vegetable oil for deep-frying

2 handfuls of sorrel leaves, washed and drained

2 heads of chicory

a handful of curly parsley, stems removed

a very small handful of capers (extra-fine if possible)

Vinaigrette (see page 253)

This is a fine accompaniment for Brawn (see opposite).

Allow the boiled ears to cool and firm up, then slice very thinly. Heat the vegetable oil in a deep frying pan (or deep fryer if you have one) and drop the ears in. Be careful, as even if dry they are likely to spit. Stir to avoid them sticking in one great mass. When crispy remove from the oil and lay on kitchen paper to drain off excess fat.

Pick the sorrel leaves from the stems, chop the chicory and finely chop the curly parsley, add the capers, dress with a vinaigrette, and then top with the crispy ear.

PRESSED PIG'S EAR

To serve eight to ten as a starter

14 pigs' ears, cleaned and any remaining hair shaved off with a Bic razor, then brined for at least 3 days (see page 269)

3 pigs' trotters, cleaned

2 onions, peeled

2 carrots, peeled

2 leeks, cleaned

2 sticks of celery

1 head of garlic

a bundle of parsley, thyme and rosemary

2 bay leaves

black peppercorns

enough very light chicken stock to cover the above ingredients

This is as close as it gets to turning a sow's ear into a silk purse. One could be forgiven for thinking of ears as rubbery things, not blessed with much culinary potential. Well, think again!

Pigs' ears are not expensive so don't be shy; ask your butcher, who should have no problem getting them, as where there are pigs there must be ears. If you have to amass your ears over a few days, do not worry, as this is where your brine bucket will come in handy.

Remove the ears from the brine, rinse thoroughly and soak in fresh water for half a day. Final ear procedure: you need to flatten them, so when they turn into funnels split them open with a knife.

Place all the ingredients in a pot and cover with the chicken stock, then lid on pot and into a medium oven for 4 hours. After 3 hours, take a look; remember you want a totally submissive texture, but also that there is the cartilage in the ear, which will never give in.

When done, remove from the oven. Carefully take out the ears and layer them in a terrine mould or bread tin lined with cling film. Strain the liquor off the vegetables and trotters into a clean pan. Place on the hob and simmer until reduced to the point where it will still cover the ears. Check for seasoning – remember it is going to be served cold, which always dulls flavour.

Pour the reduced liquor over the ears. Cut a bit of cardboard to fit in your mould, cover it with cling film and place on top of your juicy ears. Apply weights to it – tins of tomato etc. Allow to cool, then leave in the fridge overnight. Next day it is ready to eat.

Turn the pressed pigs' ears out of the container and slice very thinly with a very sharp knife. What you should have now is thin slivers of joyous piggy jelly, within which there is a beautiful weave of ear. When you bite into it, you should have that splendid textural moment of the give of the jelly and the slightest crunch of the ear cartilage. Serve with cornichons.

BATH CHAPS

Bath chaps are a speciality of the West Country, and if you have a spirited butcher he will prepare them for you wherever you are, if asked nicely. They are a boned-out pig's head which is rolled so the tongue is in the centre, surrounded by the cheeks and their protective layer of fat, and tapering to one end where you have the nozzle.

This should be brined for 3 days (see page 269), then boiled in a similar fashion to the whole head (see page 88), though 2 hours' cooking time should be ample, not having the skull to contend with. You can then slice it and serve it hot, with mash and Green Sauce as with the cheek and tongue on page 86; or allow it to go cold, slice it thinly and eat it with gherkins; or fry slices, which are delicious served with greens tossed in a Mustard Dressing (see page 257).

PIG'S HEAD AND POTATO PIE

To serve six

1 pig's head (it might be more manageable to ask your butcher to saw it in half)

2 onions, peeled

2 carrots, peeled

2 sticks of celery

2 leeks

1 head of garlic

a bundle of thyme, bay leaf and parsley stalks

a handful of black peppercorns, confined in a muslin pouch

½ bottle of white wine

enough light chicken stock to cover the head

Puff Pastry (see page 231)

1.5kg potatoes such as Maris Piper, peeled and cut into slices 2mm thick

a bunch of sage, leaves plucked from the stem and finely chopped

12 cloves of garlic, peeled and finely chopped

sea salt and black pepper

This is the pie we proudly served for lunch to celebrate The Top Fifty Restaurants in the World. This is no humble pie.

Place the head in a pan large enough to accommodate it. Add the vegetables, bundle of herbs, pepper pouch and white wine. Cover with stock, bring to the boil, then simmer for 3 hours. Check with a sharp knife – you want the flesh to come away from the bone without resistance. When it is giving, remove the head from the pan and, while still warm, pluck the flesh from the skull. Chop this into half-walnut-sized chunks.

Butter a 30cm springform cake tin and lay greaseproof paper on the bottom. Roll out the puff pastry to approximately 8mm thick and use to line the tin. Starting with potato, fill the pie with alternate layers of potato and head. To complete each head layer, add the finely chopped sage, garlic and some salt and pepper. Slightly overfill your pie to allow for the inevitable slumping. Cover with a lid of pastry, on top of which put an ovenproof plate to weight it down.

Place in a medium oven and bake for at least 2 hours. It is vital that the potatoes are cooked, so check with a skewer. When you are happy, remove the pie from the oven and leave it for 10 minutes, so it can adjust to its new status. Then remove the plate, pop off the tin and serve. Express yourself with whatever accompaniment, but the pie speaks red wine to me.

PIG'S HEAD AND BEANS

Should feed approximately six

1 pig's head – remove any
unwanted hair with a Bic razor

2 carrots, peeled

2 onions, cut in half

2 heads of garlic

2 sticks of celery

2 leeks, slit in half lengthways
and cleaned

a handful of black peppercorns

zest of 1 lemon

a splash of red wine vinegar

½ bottle of white wine

ACCOMPANYING INGREDIENTS

2 handfuls of fresh borlotti beans,
cooked in clean water with
2 heads of garlic

6 carrots, cut into long, thin slices
with a peeler

a bunch of spring onions,
cut into 1cm sections

a bunch of radishes, trimmed, but
keep the leaves if happy

2 bunches of watercress,
stalks chopped off

sea salt and black pepper

a healthy splash of red wine
vinegar

The wobble of pig's head, the starchy give of beans, the slight crunch of vegetable and the naagh of red wine vinegar, it's all there.

Place the head in a large pot with the vegetables, garlic, peppercorns, lemon zest, vinegar and wine. Cover with water, bring to a gentle boil, then reduce to a simmer. Cook for 3–4 hours, skimming as you go, until the head is totally giving and coming away easily from the bone.

Remove the head and leave until cool enough to handle, then take the meat from the skull (don't forget the tongue). Meanwhile, strain the cooking liquor into a clean pan and reserve.

Cut the meat into walnut-sized chunks and return them to the pan of cooking liquor. Add the beans and allow them to bond emotionally but not physically on the heat. When you feel there is the appropriate rapport between head and beans, add the other ingredients, seasoning to taste with salt, pepper and the vinegar. Allow your vegetables time to wilt but not cook, so that you have the wobble of head with the gentle resistance of the wilting veg and the reassuring bean element, all captured in a puddle on the plate. Serve immediately.

WARM PIG'S HEAD
To feed four

1 pig's head and rest of ingredients for Brawn (see page 88), except trotters

2 bunches of wild rocket with stems trimmed off (if not available replace them with watercress or other green peppery leaves)

a bunch of sorrel leaves, picked from the stems

a big handful of curly parsley, finely chopped

a handful of cornichons, chopped

a handful of whole extra-fine capers

a handful of chunks of yesterday's white bread

DRESSING

extra virgin olive oil

2 tsp Dijon mustard

a healthy splash of red wine vinegar

2 cloves of garlic, crushed

sea salt and black pepper

The flesh from a pig's head is flavoursome and tender. Consider, its cheeks have had just the right amount of exercise and are covered in just the right enriching layer of fat to ensure succulent cooking results, and the nozzle has the lip-sticking quality of not being quite flesh nor quite fat, the perfect foil to the crunch of the crispy ear.

Cook the head as for Brawn except without the trotters. Cut the ears off so they can be rescued from the pot if there is any sign of the flesh falling off the cartilage. As soon as they're done, remove them from the pot, allow them to cool and firm up, then slice very thinly and fry as on page 89. Test the pig's head with a knife, and when the cheeks are coming away from the bone, remove it from the pot.

While still hot, remove the flesh from the pig's skull, peel and slice the tongue, and shred the meat. Then dress and toss with the other ingredients and top off with the crispy ear and serve while still warm.

POT-ROAST HALF PIG'S HEAD
To serve two

a dollop of duck fat

8 shallots, peeled and
left whole

8 cloves of garlic, peeled
and left whole

½ pig's head (your butcher should
have no problems supplying this)
– remove any hairs with a razor

1 glass of brandy

a bundle of joy –
thyme, parsley and a
little rosemary

½ bottle of white wine

chicken stock

sea salt and black pepper

a healthy spoonful of
Dijon mustard

a bunch of watercress, trimmed,
or other greens – a case of
expressing yourself

I say only half a head, as it is a perfect romantic supper for two. Imagine gazing into the eyes of your loved one over a golden pig's cheek, ear and snout.

Dollop the duck fat into an oven tray wide and deep enough to accommodate your half a pig's head and put it on the heat. Add the shallots and garlic and leave them to do a little sweating to improve the flavour of the dish. Shuggle the tin occasionally to prevent any burning, but you do want some colour.

When happy with these, cover the ear of your demi-head with foil so that it doesn't frazzle, then rest the head in the tin. To welcome it to its new environment, pour the glass of brandy over it, nustle in your bundle of joy, add the wine and then the chicken stock. What we are looking for is the half pig's head to lurk in the stock in a not dissimilar fashion to an alligator in a swamp.

Season with salt and pepper, cover the tin with greaseproof paper, offering some protection but not denying the need for the rigours of the hours to come in the oven – which is where you should now put your tin, in a medium oven for 3 hours, until the head is totally giving. Check it after 2–2½ hours; you could remove the greaseproof paper at this point and get a little colour on your cheek.

When ready, remove the head to a warm place. Whisk the Dijon mustard into the pan liquor, in which you should then wilt the bunch of watercress.

Finally, on the head presentation platter, make a pillow of shallots, garlic and wilted watercress, where you then rest your head. There you have it, dinner for two; open something red and delicious: Moon, June, Spoon.

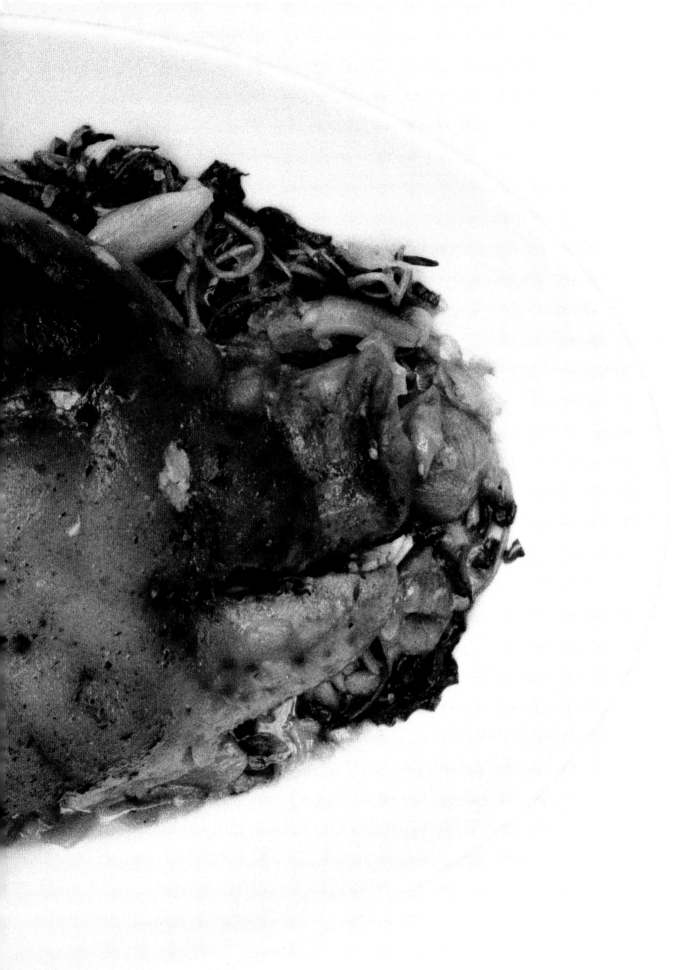

PIG'S TROTTER
STUFFED WITH POTATO

To serve four

4 long pig's trotters

sea salt

stock vegetables and herbs (what you have to hand)

1 head of garlic, separated into cloves

½ bottle of red wine

1.35kg good mashing potatoes (e.g. Maris Piper)

2 shallots, peeled and sliced

duck fat or extra virgin olive oil

black pepper

caul fat (your butcher should have no problem obtaining this for you)

A good addition to this dish is very finely chopped, blanched green cabbage mixed into your mash as well as shallots, so you are stuffing your trotter with a bubble and squeak.

Singe all the hair off the trotters, then bone them out. Chefs have likened this to being as easy as removing a kid glove, but if you don't find this, don't get disheartened. Start at the other end from the hoof, cut under the skin as close to the bone as possible (avoid cutting through the skin), work your knife further down the trotter following the bone round, you should get down to the first *claws*! Now roll the skin down the trotter towards the nails, you come to the two nails sticking out to the side, cut these at the join so they stay part of your trotter skin, ease the skin down a wee bit further to the main joint, before the *cloven hooves*!! Give this a firm bend until it cracks, and finish splitting with a knife. Sprinkle the trotter skins with salt and put them in the fridge.

Pop the bones into a pot with your stock vegetables and herbs, and cover with water. Bring them to the boil and simmer for 2½ hours, skimming regularly. When done, strain the liquor, and discard the bones and vegetables.

Shake the salt off the trotters and lay them in an oven tray. Nestle in the cloves of garlic, and cover with a mixture of the pig's trotter stock and red wine. Cover with tinfoil and place in a medium oven. Cook for approximately 3 hours then check; it's cooked when your fingers easily meet if you pinch the trotter skin. You have to be careful at this point: you want your trotters well cooked but not collapsing! Leave to cool in the liquor, but remove before it has turned to jelly.

At this point you can put them in the fridge if you have had enough for one day, but remember to bring them out in plenty of time before the final stage to warm up, as when cold they will not be so malleable.

Meanwhile peel and cook your potatoes in salted water, until soft and ready for mashing. Drain then mash them (or put through your mouli) without adding anything. Fry your shallots in a healthy spoonful of duck fat or olive oil, until soft but not brown. Mix these and the fat into your pure mash, and season. Let this mixture cool to a handleable temperature. Fill your trotter skins with the mixture – not too full, as the potato will expand, but so as they look like whole trotters again. Then wrap each trotter in a layer of caul fat, keeping this as thin as possible. At this point it is good to let the reconstructed trotters rest overnight in the fridge.

To cook the trotters, heat an ovenproof frying pan, add a spoonful of duck fat or olive oil, season the wrapped trotters and brown them, being careful not to puncture the caul layer, then place them in a hot oven for 15–20 minutes. The caul should all but cook away, leaving a crispy trotter full of giving swollen mash, which has supped up the sticky goodness of the trotter. Eat hot with watercress.

SALTED BACK FAT AND WET WALNUTS

Rather like eating grown-up peanut butter.

Take a piece of pork back fat (the Middle White pig has a good layer) and cover it with sea salt. Leave it in the fridge for a month. When its time is up, brush the salt off and slice very thinly onto a plate.

Crack your walnuts open and extract the nuts. Break into pieces over the plated back fat.

Eat with fingers, rolling the back fat around some walnut and popping it in your mouth.

DRIED SALTED PIG'S LIVER, RADISHES AND BOILED EGGS

To serve eight

LIVER

500g sea salt

500g sugar

1 pig's liver

a handful of ground black pepper

SALAD

a bunch of radishes (preferably breakfast radishes), washed, and their leaves (if the leaves are not happy then rocket, preferably wild, will substitute)

4 x 8-minute boiled eggs, peeled and chopped in halves or quarters

8 spring onions (roll in a hot pan with some oil so they begin to soften as they act as a structural weave through the salad)

a handful of capers (extra-fine if possible)

a handful of chopped curly parsley

a splash of Vinaigrette (see page 253)

a smidgen of extra virgin olive oil

a splash of balsamic vinegar

This may sound hardcore but it is as balanced as a salad can be.

LIVER

Find a plastic, glass, or china container that will fit in your fridge and is large enough for the liver. Mix the salt and sugar and lay a healthy layer in your container. Rub the mix into the liver's nooks and crannies, then lay it on your prepared bed. Cover the liver with the remaining mix, cover it with a lid or cling film, and leave in the fridge for 2 weeks (if the mixture all melts away with the juices from the liver, you may have to replenish with more dry mixture).

When the time is up, remove the liver from the mixture: it should be firm but not rock hard. Rinse it thoroughly with cold water. Dry it with a clean cloth, rub it down with black pepper, then roll and wrap it in another clean tea towel, tying firmly with string. Leave to hang in a cool dry airy place for at least 3 weeks.

SALAD

Slice off 16 thin round slices of dried liver. Toss all the salad ingredients together in a bowl with the vinaigrette.

Get a frying pan hot and apply a drop of oil. Place the liver slices in – your aim is to simply show them the pan – then turn them over, apply a healthy splash of balsamic vinegar, and allow them to sizzle for a moment. Remove from the heat; the liver slices should be shimmering and slightly softened. Lay them on top of the salad, drizzle the remaining juices from the pan on top and serve immediately.

ROLLED PIG'S SPLEEN

Per person

1 pig's spleen (given prior warning your butcher should have no problem obtaining it)

sea salt and black pepper

4 sage leaves

2 slices of smoked streaky bacon, not too thin, rind removed

chicken stock, enough to cover the spleen

People venting their spleens have been a bad press gastronomically for the organ. Please do not be deterred; spleens are a joy to cook with and eat, and the texture is not dissimilar to liver.

Lay your spleen out flat (it is a very neat and easy to use organ) and season. Place your sage leaves along it, then the bacon lengthwise, roll it up, and skewer it. Place in an ovenproof dish, cover with the chicken stock, put in a medium oven for 1½ hours, then let it cool in the stock. When cold it is ready to eat; you can keep it in the stock until you need it.

To serve, remove the skewer, cut into three or four slices (so you get a cross-section of spleen and bacon spiral), and eat with very thinly sliced raw red onion and cornichons.

ROAST PORK LOIN, TURNIPS, GARLIC AND ANCHOVIES

To serve six

about 2.5kg pork loin on the bone
*(you will want 6 chops out of it at
the end) – ask the butcher to chine
it and not to score the skin*

2 onions, peeled and chopped

sea salt and black pepper

*18 cloves of garlic with skin on,
separated, roasted in the oven
until soft and sweet, then squeezed
out of their skins and mashed*

*1 small tin of anchovies in oil,
drained and finely chopped*

*a handful of capers
(extra-fine if possible)*

a handful of curly parsley, chopped

*a healthy splash of extra virgin
olive oil*

a splash of red wine vinegar

*12 small or 6 large turnips, peeled
and chopped, turnip greens
reserved – if there are none,
rocket makes a good substitute*

Is it not splendid when you have a guest to stay who cooks delicious things for you? A fine example is Ken, a chef from Sydney, who prepared this dish full of most of my favourite things. He even finished it off with a healthy splash of truffle oil, which I have omitted from this version, but please express yourself.

Remove the skin of the pork in one piece (this is not hard: with a thin sharp knife, gently slice under the skin, following it around the pork), then gently score it (if in doubt your butcher will remove it and score it for you). Place the skin back where it was before. In a roasting tray lay out your onions and place your pork and skin on top of them, then season. Put into a hot oven for 2½ hours.

Meanwhile, make your dressing: mix the garlic, anchovies, capers, parsley, oil, vinegar and pepper, and keep at the ready. Fifteen minutes before the pork is done cook your turnips in boiling salted water. When cooked add the greens then drain straight away. Place these into a serving bowl, dress, and toss so all get to know the dressing. Remove the pork from the oven; it will hold its heat well and will enjoy a rest if things are a little out of synch.

If the skin is not crispy enough return it to the oven to crisp up while you slice the loin into chops. Place these on top of the dressed turnips and greens. Finally, remove the crisp skin from the oven and roughly chop it with a big knife. Top the dish off with this and serve.

BEANS AND BACON

*To feed four, but can easily expand and is a good dish for many hearty
eaters on a cold day, so go as big as your pot allows you (on a cold day)*

*1kg white haricot beans,
soaked overnight*

*1 pig's trotter (2 litres chicken
stock will be splendid if
no trotter is available)*

2 carrots, peeled

2 onions, peeled

2 sticks of celery

3 heads of garlic

*a bundle of thyme, rosemary
and parsley*

*1kg piece of good green streaky
bacon with skin on*

duck fat or extra virgin olive oil

3 onions, peeled and chopped

2 leeks, peeled and chopped

1 tin of plum tomatoes

sea salt and black pepper

'Landlord, bring us beans and bacon and a bottle of your finest
Burgundy.'

Put the beans into a pan with clean water, bring to the boil, skim,
and reduce to a simmer until thoroughly giving. This will take
approximately 1½ hours. As soon as they meet the salty bacon they
will stop getting any softer, in fact they seem to firm up (many recipes
suggest soaking and blanching for 10 minutes is enough, but in my
experience, once they meet salt – however long you cook them for –
they never give in). Once cooked, remove from the heat, but keep
them in their liquor.

Separately cover your trotter with water, add the carrots, whole
onions, celery, 1 head of garlic and the herbs, and bring to the boil.
Skim, reduce to a simmer, and cook for 2½ hours.

While all this is happening, remove the skin from the piece of bacon,
if possible in one piece, and slice the bacon into 8mm thick slices.

Get a deep pan hot and add a healthy dollop of duck fat (or oil). Firstly
fry the piece of bacon skin, fat down, so it releases some of its fat into
the pan, and remove; then colour your bacon slices and remove;
then fry your chopped onions and leeks until softened, and add the
tin of tomatoes, crushing the tomatoes in your hands as you do so.
Let this cook down for 20 minutes to sweeten the tomatoes, stirring
to remove all the good bits of bacon that might adhere to the pan,
season, remembering the bacon is salty, add two ladles of the trotter
stock, and let cook for another 10 minutes. Drain the beans but keep
their liquor, add to the pan, and mix with the tomato base.

Now for the final construction. Find a thick pot with a lid which will fit all your ingredients. At the bottom of the pot lay your bacon skin, fat down, then a layer of your saucy beans, strips of bacon, beans, a nestled trotter and 2 heads of garlic, beans, bacon, beans and so on …

When everything is in place, top up with trotter stock to just cover the beans (if this runs out, use the bean juice or chicken stock). Cover and put in a medium to hot oven for 1½ hours, then uncover and cook for a further 30 minutes until a crustiness forms on the top. Serve hot from the pot on the table with much red wine.

BACON KNUCKLE AND PICKLED CABBAGE

Serves four and should leave you with cabbage left over for future use

2 white cabbages

100g coarse sea salt

20 juniper berries

4 smallish firm onions, peeled and thinly sliced

a good spoonful of duck fat

10 black peppercorns

3 bay leaves

600g piece of good smoked pork belly or smoked streaky bacon, skin removed and sliced into four

4 smoked bacon knuckles

1 bottle of dry white wine

If you omit the knuckles and up the bacon quota, the resulting cabbage makes a very good accompaniment to pheasant or pigeon.

Slice the cabbage finely with a good big knife. Find a china, glass or plastic container, which will not react with the salt (aluminium is not appropriate). Put in a layer of chopped cabbage, salt and juniper berries, then cabbage again. Continue to fill the container in this fashion then cover with a weighted lid. Leave somewhere warmish for 2 weeks. It will produce lots of water and when you smell it, it will smell quite *umpfy*. This is all good.

After 2 weeks, release your cabbage from its weights and rinse thoroughly. Get a thick pot, in which you cook down your onions in the duck fat. When they are happy and soft, not brown, take off the heat. Put in a healthy layer of pickled cabbage, sprinkle on the peppercorns and bay leaves, then nestle the pork belly or bacon and knuckles into the cabbage. Cover with more cabbage, pour your bottle of wine over this, lay on it the bacon skin, fat down, and cover tightly with tinfoil and a lid. Pop into a gentle oven and cook for 2–3 hours until the knuckles are soft and giving.

Serve with boiled potatoes.

BOILED BELLY
AND LENTILS
To serve four

BOILED BELLY

*2kg piece of pork belly, with
skin and bones on, which has
been in a brine for 10 days
(see page 269), rinsed*

2 whole carrots, peeled

*2 onions, peeled and stuck
with 8 cloves*

2 leeks, whole and cleaned

2 sticks of celery

2 whole heads of garlic

a bunch of fresh herbs

black peppercorns

LENTILS

extra virgin olive oil

*1 onion, peeled and chopped
into thin slices*

*1 leek, cleaned and chopped
into thin slices*

*5 cloves of garlic, peeled
and chopped finely*

*2 carrots, peeled and chopped in
half, then into 5mm thick slices*

500g Puy lentils

a bundle of thyme and parsley

sea salt and black pepper

*a big handful of chopped
curly parsley*

**This dish celebrates the not quite meat, not quite fat, quality
of pork belly.**

BOILED BELLY

Place the pork belly into a pan with all the other ingredients, and
cover with water. Bring to the boil, skim, and reduce to a very gentle
simmer with the water barely moving for 3½ hours, until the flesh
is soft and giving, but not collapsing. Remove from the water, slice,
and serve with lentils and mustard.

Encourage your dining companions to eat the fat and all. With the
rich and fatty belly you want quite dour lentils.

LENTILS

Cover the bottom of a largish pan with olive oil, and sweat your
chopped vegetables and garlic. At the moment they are only just
starting to soften, not colouring, add the lentils. Stir these for a
couple of minutes in the oil and vegetables, then cover with water and
nestle in the thyme and parsley bundle. Simmer and stir occasionally
– you want the lentils soft but not squidgy, so that they have reserved
their lentil integrity, but are not still individual hard nuts. This should
take about 40 minutes. If they dry out add a spot more water.

Now season, which, particularly with lentils, is a very exciting
moment. It is amazing what simple salt and pepper do to the flavour
of lentils – they make lentils of them. Just before serving, stir in your
chopped parsley and a healthy splash of extra virgin olive oil which will
enrich and give a shine to your lentils, as they can veer to the dull side.

BRINED PORK BELLY, ROASTED

To serve four

a brine (see page 269)

2kg piece of pork belly, with skin and bones on

2 onions, peeled and chopped

a minuscule splash of extra virgin olive oil

a pinch of coarse sea salt

Delicious and cheap cut of pig.

Brine your pork belly piece for 3 days, rinse, then score the skin gently with a sharp knife (a Stanley knife is excellent for this purpose).

Place the onions on the base of a roasting tray (their purpose is, as well as flavour, to stop the belly sticking). Lay the belly on top. Rub the skin with a little oil and then the salt. Place in a medium to hot oven for approximately 1½–2 hours; keep an eye on it so it does not burn. If you're anxious that the skin is not crisping up, you can start or finish the belly under the grill.

When cooked you should have crispy skin on top of soft and giving fatty flesh. Lift off the onions and serve.

BOILED HAM AND PARSLEY SAUCE

To serve four

2kg piece of rolled green
collar of good ham

2 sticks of celery

2 onions, peeled and stuck
with 8 cloves

2 leeks, cleaned

3 bay leaves

10 black peppercorns

10 good-sized carrots, peeled
but left whole; this way they
stay sweeter

PARSLEY SAUCE

100g butter

100g plain white flour

600ml milk

sea salt and black pepper

a big bunch of curly parsley,
finely chopped

Incredibly simple, but delicious and particularly beautiful on the plate. I believe it is important to have the parsley sauce in a jug on the table so the eaters can express themselves with their pouring. When buying your ham, avoid pink things in hair nets, look for organic and free range if possible. It is always good to cook a bit more than you will eat so you can have cold ham.

Place your ham in a pot, keeping in mind you will need room for your carrots. Cover with water, add the celery, onions, leeks, bay leaves and peppercorns. Bring gently to the boil, skim, reduce to a simmer for 2½ hours. Add your carrots.

Now make your sauce. Melt the butter in a pan, add the flour, and stir on a gentle heat – do not let it colour, it's ready for the milk when it smells biscuity. Add the milk, whisking ferociously, making sure the heat's not too fierce. When you have a firm white creamy mixture, add a ladle of ham stock, and whisk again. Do this until you have reached your desired consistency. Test for seasoning. Just before serving add the chopped parsley and stir.

When the carrots are cooked you are ready to serve (if the ham is cooked and the carrots not, remove the ham from the water and turn up the heat). Slice the ham and serve on a plate with carrots and a drizzle of ham stock from the pot. Mustard is vital on the table.

You will be left with delicious ham stock for another day, and cold ham for your sandwiches.

BROAD BEANS, HAM AND PARSLEY SAUCE

yesterday's boiled ham, cut into chunks

broad beans

Parsley Sauce (see previous page)

The most delicious way of using up the remaining boiled ham, in fact so good it is worth boiling ham especially for the dish.

Gently warm the chunks of ham in the water it was boiled in yesterday. Boil the broad beans in the ham broth. When cooked (approximately 3 minutes), drain and place in a dish, nestle the warm ham into the beans, pour hot parsley sauce on the ham and beans, and eat straight away. A joy!

HAM IN HAY

This will feed twelve (though if you are fewer, what better than to have some left over cold?)

a big bundle of hay (organic, for obvious reasons)

10 juniper berries

14 black peppercorns

10 cloves

6 bay leaves

1 leg of green gammon (hind leg, unsmoked bacon, with bone in)

The cooking of ham in hay imbues it with the most wonderful and unusual flavour, while insulating the meat from any fierce heat so that it cooks in the ideal gentle fashion, resulting in the most giving of flesh. It also fills your home with rustic, pastoral smells. To obtain your hay ask a friendly farmer if one is to hand or just ask around – this can have surprisingly productive results. If all else fails a reliable pet shop is a good source.

You will need a pot large enough to fit a leg of bacon!

In a big pot make a base of hay, sprinkle on your spices and bay leaves, and lay the ham in your hay nest. Cover with more hay around and on top. Cover with water. Bring to the boil then straight away turn down to the gentlest simmer. Put a lid on and cook either in the oven or on top, making sure that it is not boiling too fast. Cook until tender all the way through, check by probing with a thin sharp knife; it will take 3½–4½ hours. The hay is sadly not edible.

Serve with swede mash (if possible made with goose or duck fat). The pink ham and the orange swede look like a sunset on a plate.

CURED HAM

For one boned but not rolled collar of pork

STAGE ONE

2 bottles of red wine

1 tbsp saltpetre (if available – be careful, it is very strong and itches terribly if it comes in contact with the skin) or 400g sea salt

12 whole cloves

2 heads of garlic, cut in half to expose the flesh of the bulbs

12 peppercorns

STAGE TWO

1.2kg sea salt and 800g sugar, mixed together

This recipe has its origins in the Italian method for making *coppa*, but has been handed on in a verbal fashion from an Italian prisoner-of-war who took up residence in France to my previous sous-chef, Paul Hughes, then to me and now to these pages. Inevitably there is an element of Chinese whispers, with the recipe changing accordingly, so what we have here may not relate at all to how Italians make *coppa*, but it makes a fine cured ham.

Mix all the ingredients for stage one together in a container made of glass, plastic or china, and immerse your pork collar in the mixture. It is vital the collar is covered. Place in the fridge for 12 days.

Now remove the collar from its winey bath and dry thoroughly with a clean tea towel. Wash out your container thoroughly and dry it. Now lay some wooden strips along the bottom of the container which will lift your pork off the bottom (chopsticks are very good for this).

Rub the salt mixture for stage two into the pork, then lay it in the container on your waiting slats. Pack the rest around and on top of the collar and return it to the fridge for 2 weeks. If the salt and sugar become wet and run off the pork, make up another mix and reapply.

Stage three requires good strong arms, strong kitchen string and muslin or stockinet cloth. A fortnight has passed and it is time to remove the collar from the container, rinse with cold water, and dry thoroughly. Now forcefully roll your collar and tie tightly; this is vital for the prevention of internal mould. Wrap in the cloth and hang somewhere cool, airy and dry for 2 months, by which point it should be ready to slice.

I am afraid this recipe is not failsafe; nature being nature, mould and rot can strike, but please do not let this deter you as when it works it is delicious and well worth the effort and patience.

CRISPY PIGS' TAILS

To serve four

8 long pigs' tails

2 onions, peeled and
roughly chopped

2 carrots, peeled and
roughly chopped

2 sticks of celery, chopped

10 black peppercorns

a bundle of fresh herbs

3 bay leaves

1 head of garlic

zest of 1 lemon

½ bottle of red wine

1.1 litres chicken or light stock

2 tbsp English mustard

4 eggs, whisked together

450g seasoned flour

225g fine white breadcrumbs

a large knob of butter

**On other pages I have sung the praises of how the pig's snout
and belly both have that special lip-sticking quality of fat and flesh
merging, but this occurs in no part of the animal as wonderfully
as on the tail. You must ask your butcher for long tails.**

Place the tails in an oven dish with the vegetables, peppercorns,
herbs, garlic, lemon zest and wine, and cover with the stock. Cover
with tinfoil, place in a medium oven, and cook for 3 hours, checking
on it so it does not cook too fast; when done you should be able to
easily pinch through the flesh. Remove from the oven. Allow to cool
in the stock, but remove the tails before it turns to jelly and drain any
excess liquid off them (you can refrigerate them at this point).

When they're cold and firm, mix together the mustard and eggs
and have ready three bowls: flour, egg and mustard, and breadcrumbs.
Dust them with flour, roll them in the egg and mustard mix, and
finally coat them in the breadcrumbs so that they are well covered
(do this just before you cook, otherwise the crumbs will go soggy).

Get a large ovenproof frying pan or roasting tray hot, add the butter,
and when sizzling add the tails and roll them around (watch out, they
can and will spit – be very careful). Place in a hot oven for 10 minutes,
then turn them over, making sure there is enough butter, and roast for
another 10 minutes, keeping an eye on them so they do not burn.

Serve hot with watercress or red mustard salad. Some may like a
spot of malt or red wine vinegar on their tails. Encourage the use
of fingers and much gnawing of the bone.

BLOOD CAKE AND FRIED EGGS

Makes one cake, which should easily feed eight

1 large or 2 small onions, peeled and finely chopped

6 cloves of garlic, finely chopped

a dollop of duck fat

half a bunch of marjoram – pick the leaves off and chop finely

½ tsp crushed mace

½ tsp crushed allspice

1 litre fresh pig's blood

150g yellow cornmeal (polenta)

sea salt and black pepper

250g back fat (salted lardo will suffice), cut into 5mm cubes

16 free-range eggs

You will need to ask your butcher for the blood. It may be difficult to obtain, but it can be got. We have found the blood from the Gloucester Old Spot to be the sweetest. You will also need a bread tin lined with cling film.

In a pan large enough to take all the ingredients, sweat the onions and garlic in the duck fat until clear, soft and giving, but not brown. Add the marjoram, spices, blood and cornmeal, and stir on a gentle heat until the blood starts to thicken to a running porridge consistency (do not let it cook and set). It has to have a certain density or the back fat will sink to the bottom when added. At this point (not for the more squeamish cook) taste and adjust the seasoning with salt and pepper if necessary, and when happy remove the pan from the heat and add the chopped back fat.

Stir to spread the fatty chunks through the blood and decant the mixture into the cling-film-lined bread tin. Cover with tinfoil and place on a flat folded tea towel in a deep roasting tray or dish. Surround with water (not going over the edge of the bread tin) and bake in a gentle to medium oven for 1½ hours. Check that a skewer or sharp knife comes out clean, then remove and allow to cool and set (wrapped in cling film it keeps very well in the fridge).

Once firm, cut into 12mm thick slices, get two frying pans hot, add some duck fat to them, and gently fry your slices of blood cake until heated through. In the other pan, fry a pair of eggs per person. To serve, give each plate two slices of fried blood cake, topped with a couple of fried eggs, and eat straight away. It has surprising soothing qualities, this dish.

TO DINING

ROAST WHOLE SUCKLING PIG

1 appropriately sized piglet

extra virgin olive oil

sea salt and black pepper

STUFFING

4 red onions, peeled and sliced

a dollop of duck fat

½ bottle of red wine

the kidneys from the pig, chopped

about ½ loaf of yesterday's white bread

sea salt and black pepper

2 cloves of garlic, peeled and crushed

8 sage leaves, chopped

It's very important to keep in mind the size of your oven when purchasing your suckling pig. There is nothing sadder than a wee pig ready to roast and it won't fit in the oven. So …

Cook the red onions in the duck fat until completely tender. Pour in the red wine. Let this simmer and reduce until you have a *moving* marmalade of red onion. Add the chopped-up kidneys from the piglet and some chunks of yesterday's white bread. Season and stir. At this point you should have a mass of bread cubes held together by an onion weave. Take off the heat and add the garlic and sage to the mix.

Now stuff your piglet, rather like those cuddly animals you kept your pyjamas in. The stuffing will swell, being designed to be receptive of all the piggy juices, so some rudimentary sewing up of the pig is required.

Sit the pig on an oven tray in a sphinx-like manner, then rub some oil onto it as if it is Ambre Solaire on a good friend's back. Season liberally and place in a medium oven for 3–4 hours. You want a pig at the end that offers no resistance to your carving. Gather friends and have a feast.

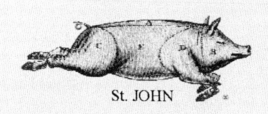

TROTTER GEAR

UNCTUOUS POTENTIAL

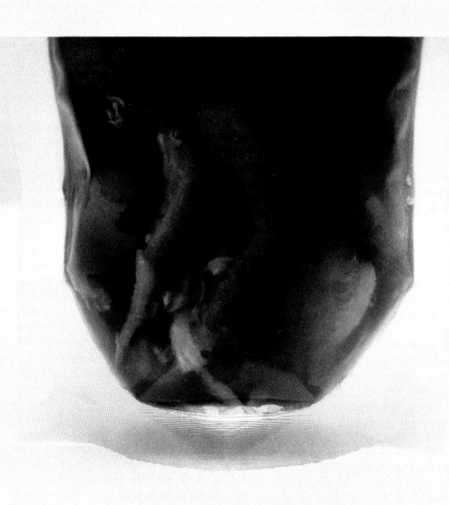

TROTTER GEAR

(Unctuous potential)

RECIPE FOR A HEALTHY JAR OF TROTTER GEAR
GUINEA FOWL, RED CABBAGE, TROTTER AND PRUNE
POT-ROAST BACON, TROTTER AND PRUNE
BACON, TROTTER AND PRUNE ON FOIE GRAS TOAST
BEEF AND PICKLED WALNUT STEW
SNAIL, TROTTER, SAUSAGE AND CHICKPEAS
BRAISED SQUIRREL
DEEP-FRIED RABBIT
GAME PIE

RECIPE FOR A HEALTHY JAR OF TROTTER GEAR

Makes one healthy jar

6 pigs' trotters, all hair removed (a disposable Bic razor can prove very useful at this moment)

2 onions, peeled

2 carrots, peeled

2 sticks of celery

2 leeks, slit in half lengthways and cleaned

1 head of garlic

a bundle of thyme

a handful of black peppercorns

½ bottle of Sercial Madeira

enough chicken stock to cover the trotters

This unctuous, giving gastronomic tool will become all chefs' and cooks' friend, finding untold uses in the kitchen. No fridge should be without its jar of Trotter Gear.

Place the trotters in a large casserole. Cover with water and bring to the boil. Boil for 5 minutes, then drain. This removes the initial scum given off by the trotters.

Now place the blanched trotters back in the pot with the vegetables, garlic, thyme, peppercorns and Madeira and cover with stock. Cover and place in a gentle oven. Cook for at least 3 hours, until the trotters are totally giving. At this point, strain the cooking liquor and keep. When the trotters have cooled enough to handle (but don't let them go cold, as they become much harder to deal with), pick all the flesh, fat and skin off them, tearing the skin into shreds. Add to the cooking liquor, seal in a jar and refrigerate.

You now have Trotter Gear, nuduals of giving, wobbly trotter captured in a splendid jelly. One can sense its potential even now.

GUINEA FOWL, RED CABBAGE, TROTTER AND PRUNE

Each guinea fowl will feed two to three people, depending on their appetite

1 guinea fowl – you can expand this recipe exponentially

duck fat

1 red onion, peeled and sliced

about ½ red cabbage, thinly sliced (enough to make a small nest for the bird)

4 cloves of garlic, peeled and left whole

500g Trotter Gear (see opposite)

14 Agen prunes

a bundle of thyme

2 bay leaves

2 large glasses of red wine

sea salt and black pepper

chicken stock, to cover

A most comforting sight in the middle of the table, happy bird surrounded by red cabbage, wobbly trotter and prunes. Guinea fowl could be replaced by pheasant with equally delicious results. In fact, come the winter, all the more appropriate.

Brown off your bird in duck fat, in a pan or oven tray. When appropriately tanned, remove the bird and soften the onion in the fat. Add the cabbage and garlic. Stuff the bird with some Trotter Gear and a few prunes.

Nustle the stuffed bird upside down in the cabbage and add the remaining Trotter Gear and prunes, plus the bundle of thyme, bay leaves, red wine, salt and pepper. Cover the cabbage with chicken stock. Cover the oven tray with foil and slip it into a gentle oven for 2½ hours – as always, keeping an eye on it. Check with a knife to see if you have a giving bird.

I sometimes worry about my bacon count, but this braise would happily welcome the addition of a chunk of smoked bacon.

POT-ROAST BACON, TROTTER AND PRUNE

To serve six

2 white onions, peeled and sliced

a dollop of duck fat

1 piece of smoked bacon loin (Gloucester Old Spot does very well) – cut the skin off in one piece and keep

500g Trotter Gear (see page 130)

1 large glass of white wine

22 Agen prunes, stones in

black pepper

chicken stock up your sleeve, in case a top-up is needed

This is a firm favourite. With these ingredients, how can you go wrong? Also, leftovers are good.

In a deep oven tray big enough to hold all your ingredients, sweat the onions in the duck fat until slightly softened. Place the bacon on the feathered nest, surround with Trotter Gear, and add the wine, prunes, pepper and any top-up of stock needed so that the bacon is almost covered. Lay the skin back on the bacon like a protective duvet, cover in foil and put into a medium oven for 1¾–2 hours, keeping an eye on it to make sure that nothing too ferocious is happening to it.

When ready, the prunes should have swollen with pride but maintained their dignity, thanks to their stones. Slice the bacon and serve with a hearty spoonful of trotter, onion and prune. What a joy!

BACON, TROTTER AND PRUNE ON FOIE GRAS TOAST

Sometimes great things come out of moments of adversity. At St. John Bread & Wine a foie gras terrine had not turned out as happy as we would have wished but, always thinking on our feet, we had the leftovers of Pot-Roast Bacon, Trotter and Prune …

Basic foie advice: Pull the lobes of one fresh duck's foie apart with your fingers and remove the veins. Then splash on a spot of Vieille Prune (or eau de vie of choice), toss well and cover. Pop in the fridge overnight.

Next day, get a clean Kilner jar, season your foie well with salt and toss again. Then press it into the jar, which you sit on a folded tea towel in an ovenproof dish. Surround the jar with water, lid open. Don't let any water into the jar. Place carefully in a gentle oven and keep a close eye on it. Fat will be released, which is good, but do not let your foie melt away. When happy with the state of things, remove the jar from its bath. Remember it will carry on cooking. Add the rubber seal and shut, as simple as that. When cold, pop it into the fridge.

Chop a bit of the bacon into chunks and add to the prunes and trotters (leftovers from the recipe opposite). Heat up in a pan. When hot, pour the mixture over a piece of toast on which you have spread the foie gras.

You could not wish for a more steadying, but at the same time uplifting, snack.

BEEF AND PICKLED WALNUT STEW

To serve two

1 flap off a fore rib

4 red onions, peeled and sliced

5 cloves of garlic, peeled and left whole

a bundle of thyme and rosemary

sea salt and black pepper

½ bottle of red wine

500g Trotter Gear (see page 130)

8 pickled walnuts

This is a treat for the chef who has prepared a fore rib for Sunday lunch. If you take the flap off the rib of beef, it makes an ideal piece of stewing steak.

Place the beef flap fat down in a casserole on not too high a heat – this will render some of the fat, so that you have something to cook your onions in. Remove the beef, add the onions and cook until tender. It may seem an excessive amount of onion but they give off vital acid, which will help break the beef down into a hopefully tender beast.

Return the beef to the pan with the garlic, herbs, salt, pepper, wine and Trotter Gear, which will nurture the beef, as the onions will tenderize. Now cover with foil and place in a gentle oven. After 1½ hours, add the pickled walnuts. Cook for a further 2 hours, which gives you time for a bath and a couple of dry martinis, sniffing the musk of your braised beef.

Cut into chunky slices and serve with mashed potato.

SNAIL, TROTTER, SAUSAGE AND CHICKPEAS
To serve eight

400g dried chickpeas, soaked in
cold water overnight

2 heads of garlic

12 shallots, peeled and left whole

a splash of extra virgin olive oil

some green bacon chunks
(you can never fit in enough
pork with a pulse)

12 cloves of garlic, peeled
and left whole

500g Trotter Gear
(see page 130)

a bundle of thyme, rosemary and
parsley stalks

10 small chorizo sausages

40 fresh snails (I refer you to Tony
the Snail Man on page 23)

2 bunches of rocket

Vinaigrette (see page 253)

sea salt and black pepper

A steady *bowl* affair, this should bring comfort to many on a cold day.

Drain the chickpeas, cover with fresh water and add the heads of garlic. Bring to the boil, then cook at a gentle simmer for about 3 hours – you want totally submissive chickpeas or the giving nature of the dish will be lost.

Gently brown off the shallots in the oil, then add the green bacon. Allow to sizzle, then add the garlic cloves, Trotter Gear, bundle of herbs and whole chorizo sausages. With a slotted spoon, add the chickpeas and any of the chickpea juice required – you are looking for a dampness.

Allow to simmer together for 20 minutes, then remove the chorizo and test the mixture for seasoning. Chop the chorizo into finger-width slices and return them to the chickpeas. Add the snails, stir and cover. Transfer to a medium-hot oven and bake for 35 minutes. When ready, chop the rocket in a disciplining fashion but don't crush it into submission. Dress it with vinaigrette and place on top of the snail/chickpea dish. The important thing to remember here is that this is a rocket top, not a garnish.

BRAISED SQUIRREL

One squirrel per person, recipe to expand as you wish

PER SQUIRREL

a dollop of duck fat

5 shallots, peeled and left whole

4 dice-sized cubes of bacon

1 glass of Vieille Prune

a handful of dried porcini mushrooms, soaked in hot water for 2 hours, then drained

2 cloves of garlic, peeled and chopped

250g Trotter Gear (see page 130)

sea salt and black pepper

chicken stock (if needed)

half a bunch of watercress, trimmed

This is a dish that strikes me as a splendid use of squirrel, which is culled by gamekeepers all over the land in February, once the game season is over but their eye is still in. With flesh like oily wild rabbit, it cooks very well and tastes delicious.

A word of warning: you may have more luck tracking your squirrels down with a rural butcher. Ask for them skinned and jointed – 2 shoulders, 2 saddle sections and 2 hind legs.

Heat up the duck fat in a large casserole and brown the whole shallots. Add the squirrel and bacon and brown the meat. Flame in the pan using the Vieille Prune. Add the soaked porcini and garlic. Allow all to sizzle for a moment, then add the Trotter Gear and some salt and pepper. If it looks dry, add some chicken stock. Cover and braise in a gentle oven for 1½ hours. Check the thigh with a sharp knife – if yielding, remove the squirrel from the casserole and wilt the watercress in it, then bring the squirrel back into the pan. It's ready.

There is something quite poetic in the way the bosky wood the squirrel inhabits has been recreated – the earthy musk of the porcini and the watercress echoing the treetops.

DEEP-FRIED RABBIT

To serve four

2 young wild rabbits, jointed
(2 shoulders, 2 saddle sections
and 2 back legs each)

500g Trotter Gear (see page 130)

chicken stock, to top up

seasoned flour

egg wash (an egg beaten with a
tiny splash of milk), with a spoonful
of Dijon mustard whisked in

very fine breadcrumbs (the fineness
is important so that you do not
end up with a bready layer
between you and your rabbit)

vegetable oil for deep-frying

lemons, cut in half

This dish is improved by the use of rabbits with youth on their side. So if you have a friend with a gun, ask them to aim for the smaller bunnies.

A deep-fat fryer is very handy for this recipe, but a pan of hot vegetable oil will suffice.

Place the jointed rabbit in a casserole, cover with the Trotter Gear and stock and place a lid or foil over the top. Put in a *gentle* oven. Cook for 2 hours but, as always, check with a sharp knife. I cannot stress gentle enough – you should have a submissive rabbit after its time, safely submerged in protective Trotter Gear. Remove the rabbit but keep the Trotter Gear, which at this point has huge flavoursome, unctuous potential.

When the rabbit is cool, dust in the seasoned flour, coat in the mustardy egg wash and then a fine layer of breadcrumbs. Deep-fry until golden. Place on kitchen paper to drain off the fat and then serve in a bowl from which everyone helps themselves, with lemon and a glass or two of something red and chirpy.

GAME PIE

To serve four with large appetites or six of a less gutsy disposition

a dollop of duck fat

450g piece of smoked bacon, skin off and kept, cut into cork-sized chunks

14 shallots, peeled but left whole

½ bottle of red wine

500g Trotter Gear (see page 130)

a spot of chicken stock up your sleeve

sea salt and black pepper

7–8cm piece of bone marrow

ANY ONE OF THE FOLLOWING

5 pigeon

5 grouse

2 pheasant

1 hare

2 wild rabbit

SUET PASTRY

250g self-raising flour

125g minced fresh beef suet

a pinch of salt

125–150ml water

1 egg, lightly beaten, to glaze

This is one of Trotter Gear's finest moments, in a game pie. This recipe could be used for pigeon, rabbit, hare, pheasant or grouse pie. Rook is another story, which I will explain later. Your game should be on the bone; if rabbit or hare, it should be jointed.

Pie-making is rather like gathering our chums together under one suet crust.

Heat up the duck fat in a deep oven tray and brown off the game, bacon and shallots. Add the red wine and allow to simmer for a moment, then add the Trotter Gear. If the ingredients are not covered entirely, top up with chicken stock. Pop the bacon skin in. Cover the tray with foil and braise in a gentle oven for about 2 hours, until the game comes away from the bone with ease. When satisfied that this is the case, allow the mixture to cool and pull the flesh off the bones. Discard the bones and tear the game meat into pie-sized pieces. This is a matter of personal taste. Return the meat to the mixture and check the seasoning.

Leave this mixture to sit overnight in the fridge, allowing it to come to terms with its new role in life and improve in flavour.

Next day find an appropriate pie dish and fill with the mixture, but not till it is falling over the edge. Nustle your piece of bone marrow into the middle of the dish so it is standing upright.

For the suet pastry, place the flour, suet and salt in a large bowl and mix together until the suet starts to break down. Then mix in enough water to make a firm paste. Wrap in cling film and leave to rest in the fridge for a few hours.

Roll out the pastry 6mm thick and use to cover the pie, moistening the rim of the dish first. Cut a hole for the bone marrow to stick through, slice off excess pastry from the sides, then press the edge down onto the moistened rim. Paint the top with the whisked egg.

It is ready for the oven, a hot oven, where it will need 35–40 minutes. Watch that the pastry does not burn; reduce the oven temperature if it starts to look too dark. There is a tempting singe and there is burnt – very different!

Let us not forget the rook. In this case bring together your pie filling as before but without the game element, until the construction of the pie, when you should slip in the raw breasts of 6 rooks; otherwise stay true to the course set before.

MEAT THAT ISN'T PIG

BOILED BEEF AND DUMPLINGS
POT-ROAST BRISKET
HASH
MINCE AND TATTIES
TRIPE AND ONIONS
GRATIN OF TRIPE
DEEP-FRIED TRIPE
BOILED OX TONGUE
TONGUE AND BEETROOT
LAMBS' TONGUES, TURNIPS AND BACON
HAGGIS
STUFFED LAMBS' HEARTS
DEVILLED KIDNEYS
LAMB'S KIDNEYS IN THEIR SUET
MUTTON AND BEANS
LAMB SHANKS EBEN'S WAY
LAMB AND BARLEY STEW
BRAISED SHOULDER OF LAMB
KID AND FENNEL

BOILED BEEF AND DUMPLINGS

To serve six

2.5kg piece of brisket (you can use silverside for this), unrolled, rinsed

a bundle of parsley and thyme

3 sticks of celery, chopped

2 bay leaves

10 black peppercorns

6 onions, peeled

6 carrots, peeled

6 leeks, cleaned

DUMPLINGS

100g suet

225g self-raising flour

a pinch of sea salt and black pepper

1 beaten egg

Boiled beef also goes remarkably well with Aïoli or Green Sauce (see pages 252 and 255), but if using these, do not include the dumplings or the pickled walnuts. To salt the briskets yourself, make a brine (see page 269) and leave them for 12 days, or you can buy salted brisket from the butcher, in which case make sure it's not rolled in.

Place your beef into a pot (remember it has to be big enough to accommodate the vegetables as well), cover with water, and add your herb bundle, celery, bay leaves and peppercorns. Bring up to the boil, skim, and reduce to a very gentle simmer, with barely signs of movement in the water, for approximately 4 hours. Prod with a knife to check how the meat feels – it should be giving, but not collapsing!

After the meat has been simmering for 2 hours put in the onions, after 2½ hours the carrots, and after 3 hours the leeks. Keep an eye on your vegetables so they do not overcook – you can always remove them. However, this is a dish that demands well-cooked vegetables, no *al dente* here. When everything is ready, remove the meat and vegetables to a serving dish and keep them warm with a splash of broth to moisten. Make the dumplings as follows.

Bring the broth to a rolling simmer. Meanwhile mix the ingredients together, adding some cold water: you are looking for quite a sticky dough. Shape into walnut-sized balls and drop into your simmering broth – they should take about 10 minutes to cook and should be like little suet clouds. Serve all together with pickled walnuts and Horseradish Sauce (see page 248).

POT-ROAST BRISKET

To serve four

2 carrots, peeled and chopped

3 onions, peeled and chopped

2 leeks, peeled and chopped

2 whole heads of garlic

a bundle of fresh herbs

10 black peppercorns

2kg piece of unrolled brisket of beef
(butchers seem very keen to roll,
just be warned), rinsed

1 litre unsalted chicken stock

2 glasses of red wine

Both this and the previous recipe provide very good leftovers for your Hash (see opposite), or are excellent in sandwiches, or simply cold, sliced thinly, with Green Sauce (see page 255) or horseradish. You can salt the brisket yourself for 5 days in a brine (see page 269) or if you don't want to make it yourself, you can buy salted brisket from the butcher.

In a deep roasting tray, just a bit bigger than your beef, lay your chopped vegetables, garlic, herbs, and pepper, onto which nestle your brisket. Pour the stock and wine over it. You are looking for an iceberg effect; part of the beef is not covered but we know there is a lot more submerged in the stock. Cover with tinfoil. Put into a medium oven for 3 hours, until thoroughly giving but not collapsing (keep an eye on it; do not let it cook too fast, and turn the oven down if this is the case).

When it's ready slice and eat the meat, ladling a little of the juice over it (keep the remaining juice, which makes a very good base for soup).

Serve with Horseradish Sauce (see page 248).

HASH

leftover brisket

oil

onions, peeled and chopped

tinned plum tomatoes

potatoes, peeled, boiled
and chopped

sea salt and black pepper

1 egg per person

A very good dish if you are feeling a little dented. This is a useful and delicious way of using up the remains of your Boiled Beef and Dumplings and Pot-Roast Brisket and (previous page and opposite). I cannot tell how much you will have left over, so we cannot be exact here. Look at your remains and decide what will be appropriate. You will need roughly the same amount of meat and veg.

Shred your cold brisket, and keep to one side. Fry the onions in oil until soft, crush a few plum tomatoes into the pan, and let these cook down. Add the potatoes and beef and season. Keep tossing in the pan until it's all heated through; if it's getting dry add some juice from the tinned tomatoes, but it is good if the potatoes get a bit of colour. Serve with a fried egg per person on top.

MINCE AND TATTIES

To serve six

1 onion, peeled and thinly sliced

1 leek, cleaned, sliced lengthways in half, then thinly sliced across

1 carrot, peeled, sliced lengthways in half, then thinly sliced across

4 cloves of garlic, peeled and chopped

a splash of extra virgin olive oil

1kg minced beef

2 tinned tomatoes

a handful of oatmeal

1 shot glass of Worcestershire sauce

⅓ bottle of red wine, my gesture to the Auld Alliance

chicken stock, if needed

sea salt and black pepper

a dozen proper boiling potatoes

A dish discussed as much as cassoulet is in Castelnaudary. Questions such as should you add peas or carrots can start a gastronomic row of great proportions. Sticking my neck out, I know Caledonia MacBrayne adds peas to its mince but I don't, although I do like a spot of carrot in mine. It gets worse – I can't help making a small gesture to the Auld Alliance as well. If you haven't tossed this book away in disgust already, here are my mince thoughts.

In a large pan, sweat the onion, leek, carrot and garlic in the splash of olive oil until softened. Add the mince, giving it a healthy stir to break it up. Add the tinned tomatoes, crushed in your hand – a subliminal gesture. Keep stirring and add the oatmeal, not so much that you end up with a porridge. Stir, add the Worcestershire sauce and red wine, then stir again. Take a view on the liquid content; if it seems a wee bit dry, add some stock. You are looking for a loose lava consistency. Check for seasoning.

Now allow the mince to simmer gently for 1½ hours, if not 2 (if it is drying out, add more stock). Time allows the mince to become itself, as is the case for most of us.

While the mince cooks, peel the potatoes and simply boil them in salty water. After a long journey, there is no dish more welcoming. Also, a dram doesn't go amiss.

TRIPE AND ONIONS
To feed four

1 litre milk

3 white onions, peeled and roughly chopped

a healthy pinch of mace blades

2kg white honeycomb tripe (which comes from the second stomach, the reticulum, of the ox), cut into 4 x 11cm strips

sea salt and black pepper

150g unsalted butter

200g plain flour

Do not let the tripe word deter you, let its soothing charms win you over and enjoy it as do those who always have!

In a pot large enough to fit all the ingredients place the milk, onions, and mace. Bring to a boil and reduce to a simmer for 20 minutes. Then add the tripe and season cautiously (you can add more seasoning later). Bring up to a gentle boil and reduce again to a simmer for a further 45 minutes to 1 hour, checking the tripe's giving qualities with a sharp knife. Be careful, as if cooked too long tripe will just melt away.

Now, in another pan, melt the butter and add the flour. Cook this, stirring to avoid browning, until it smells biscuity. Continue stirring vigorously (a whisk might be useful here) and add a couple of ladles of the liquor from the tripe pot. Once thoroughly mixed and smooth, return this mixture to the tripe. Stir in thoroughly and simmer for a further 15 minutes to allow the dish to thicken slightly. Adjust seasoning to taste and serve hot, using a slotted spoon, with mashed potato.

Visually, as well as gastronomically, there is a great serenity to a plate of tripe and onions.

GRATIN OF TRIPE

To serve four

Follow the previous recipe to its conclusion except instead of serving the Tripe and Onions with mashed potato, decant the tripe and its sauce into 4 ovenproof dishes (I think this is the only time that I recommend individual dishes, but this recipe works well this way and everyone loves their own little gratin). Cover with a layer of fine white breadcrumbs made with yesterday's bread, dot with little knobs of butter and place the dishes in a very hot oven until the tripe liquor is bubbling away. If the crust has not browned at this point, stick the dishes under the grill. When the dishes are golden brown they are ready to serve.

The eaters will each need a spoon as well as the usual tools, and advise them to stick their napkins in their collars to protect their fronts as, unlike the Tripe and Onions, which is given structure by mashed potato, so helping the journey from the plate to the mouth, tripe gratinéed, without this structural aid, is very sloppy.

DEEP-FRIED TRIPE

To serve four

a bowl of plain flour (about 250g)

a healthy pinch of cayenne pepper

a deep-fat fryer or large saucepan full of clean vegetable oil

800g cleaned and cooked white honeycomb tripe, cut into pieces not dissimilar in size to a prawn cracker

Pickled Onions (see the recipe for Pickled Shallots on page 260) and their vinegar

sea salt and black pepper

A celebration of the soothing powers of tripe, this time with a little crunch to it.

Season the flour with salt, pepper and cayenne for a little piquancy, but not enough to lose its soothing edge.

Heat the oil up in whatever cooking arrangement you have. When hot, toss the tripe in the seasoned flour, shake off excess in a sieve and slip it into the oil. Deep-fry in batches until golden. Rescue from the oil and tip onto kitchen paper to remove excess oil.

Serve immediately with pickled onion vinegar for dipping, and chips. Ahhh!

BOILED OX TONGUE

Should easily feed six people

1 salted ox tongue, rinsed

2 carrots, peeled

2 leeks, cleaned

2 onions, peeled

1 head of garlic

10 black peppercorns

2 sticks of celery

a bunch of fresh herbs

You can salt the tongue in a brine (see page 269); keep the tongue in it for 7 days. Alternatively, get a salted ox tongue from the butcher.

Cover all the ingredients with water in a pot, bring gently to the boil, and then reduce to the calmest of simmers for 3½ hours. When the tongue is cooked its skin will peel away easily; also check its givingness by stabbing it with a thin, sharp knife. Peel while still warm, as this is much easier. Tongue is a very dexterous element in a dish, and has many friends: now serve it hot or cold, grilled or fried, in a sandwich with English mustard and tomato, with a caper sauce, or with Horseradish or Green Sauce (see pages 248 and 255), and it is particularly good with beetroot, for example in Tongue and Beetroot.

TONGUE AND BEETROOT

To serve six

1.8kg fresh beetroot, whole, peel on

2 glasses of water

2 splashes of extra virgin olive oil

sea salt and black pepper

a splash of balsamic vinegar

1 cold cooked tongue (see above)

Horseradish Sauce (see page 248)

Here is true love.

In a deep roasting tray, place the beetroot, water, a splash of olive oil, salt and pepper. Cover with tinfoil and place in a hot oven for approximately 45 minutes. Check by stabbing the beetroot with a knife. Once it is done, peel the beetroot while hot (kitchen gloves help in this task) and cut into merry chunks. Dress the beetroot with oil, balsamic vinegar, salt and pepper. Serve with a thin slice of cold tongue (the beetroot starts to warm the cold tongue, loosening it) and horseradish sauce.

LAMBS' TONGUES, TURNIPS AND BACON
To serve four

STEP ONE

6 lambs' tongues (give them a rinse with cold water)

1.5 litres chicken stock

1 whole head of garlic, separated and peeled

a bundle of thyme and parsley

6 young turnips with healthy greens, chopped off but kept (if no greens, rocket makes a good substitute, or if you want something with more body, curly kale is delicious in this dish)

STEP TWO

a dollop of duck fat or butter

16 shallots, peeled and left whole

600g piece of streaky bacon, skinned and cut into chunks

sea salt and black pepper

sherry vinegar or red wine vinegar

Those little tongues.

STEP ONE

In a pan cover the lambs' tongues with the chicken stock. Add the garlic and herbs, bring to the boil, then reduce to a gentle simmer for about 2 hours, until the tongues are giving. Remove the tongues and allow to cool, until handleable, then peel while still warm. While doing this cook your turnips in the stock.

When cooked remove the turnips from the stock, take it off the heat, and return the peeled tongues to the cooling stock.

STEP TWO

In an ovenproof frying pan, melt the duck fat or butter and fry the shallots just enough to colour them. Pop them into a medium-hot oven to roast for 15 minutes, watching that they do not burn. When soft, sweet, and giving remove from the oven. Now remove the tongues from the stock and slice them in half lengthways. Heat a deep frying pan which has a lid, or a shallow saucepan. Melt a spot of duck fat or butter, fry the bacon in this so as to slightly colour it, add the tongue and turnips, allow these to colour, then add the shallots and a healthy splash of the stock to half cover the pan's contents.

Let this start to boil, then add the greens and season, then cover the pan and turn the heat down to a simmer for 2 minutes. With a slotted spoon remove ingredients to a hot deep plate, then ladle some of the liquor in the pan over, making it as dry or as brothy as you wish. Just before eating sprinkle the dish with a little vinegar.

Just as delicious, if not more so, is to substitute the turnips with broad beans (these do not need to be cooked before the final stage). You still need the rocket or kale, as the greens act as a structural weave in the dish.

155

HAGGIS

A haggis to feed six to eight

1 sheep's stomach

1 sheep's pluck, which should include the heart, lungs, windpipe, liver and some intestines

3 onions, peeled and chopped

a knob of butter

250g pinhead oatmeal, toasted (if not, bake in a flat pan in a hot oven, but don't burn or brown it)

200g prepared suet

500ml of the water the pluck was cooked in, or 500ml chicken stock

sea salt and black pepper

ground allspice

You will need a mincer.

Wash the stomach in cold water then leave to soak. Thoroughly rinse the pluck and lights in running cold water. Do not be put off by the initial look of your ingredients. Place the pluck in a large pot and cover with generously salted water. Bring to the boil then reduce to a simmer and cook for 2 hours, regularly skimming. Hang the windpipe of the pluck over the edge of your pan, with a pot underneath to catch anything the lungs may expel. Allow to cool in the liquor. Once the pluck is cold, remove it from its water and reserve 500ml of it; cut the windpipe off and discard. Cut the pluck into pieces then coarsely mince. (If the pluck did not have its windpipe, the water you have cooked the pluck in is less tempting to use to moisten your haggis in the later stages, so use the suggested alternative of chicken stock.)

Meanwhile, fry the onions in butter until soft and if the oatmeal is untoasted, toast it now.

Mix into the meat the oatmeal, suet and onions, watching the consistency, and add the cooking liquor or chicken stock. Season with salt, and particularly with pepper and allspice, and taste.

With the textural side turned inwards, find part of the stomach with no holes in it. Stuff with the mixture, and tie tightly at either end, leaving plenty of extra stomach at the outer side of the knot (when trimming off the rest of the stomach). Do not be alarmed that this looks unlike any haggis you have ever seen, and that the stomach bag looks too thick, all will be well. Wrap in tinfoil with a little kink in it to allow for expansion. Cook for 3 hours in gently simmering water.

To serve, remove from the water and tinfoil, slice it open, and spoon it out. Eat with mashed swede and mashed potatoes. In honour of the Auld Alliance, I find that Dijon mustard goes very well with haggis.

STUFFED LAMBS' HEARTS

To serve six

STUFFING

duck fat or butter

4 red onions, peeled and sliced

4 cloves of garlic, peeled and chopped

2 large glasses of red wine

225g yesterday's white bread, with crusts off, cubed

sea salt and black pepper

half a bunch of sage leaves, chopped

LAMBS' HEARTS

6 lambs' hearts (make sure they are intact, with a hole only at the top)

18 rashers of streaky bacon

1.1 litres chicken stock

In a cab home, the driver started a conversation and said 'I know you; you're the guy that cooks offal.' Here's one for you: stuffed lambs' hearts.

First make the stuffing. In a pan with duck fat or butter cook your onions and garlic gently so that they do not colour but become soft and giving. Add the wine, let this reduce by half, then add the bread, season, and cook together gently for 15 minutes: you want the stuffing to have an *unctuous* but not squidgy quality, so if it appears too dry add a splash more wine. Let the stuffing cool then add the sage.

Meanwhile trim the hearts of any excess fat nodules at their openings and any obvious sinews, and the flap at the top that looks like the bit that has a string to tighten at the top of a knapsack. Finally, with your finger, scoop out any blood clots at the base of the ventricles. You are ready to stuff.

With your hand, press the stuffing into the heart, and level off the opening at the top. Then drape 3 rashers of bacon over the exposed stuffing in a star fashion, forming a lid, and secure with string.

Find an oven dish or deep roasting tray in which the hearts will fit snugly, and stand them upright. Pour stock over them; they do not need to be completely covered but almost is good. Cover with tinfoil and place in a medium oven for 2½ hours. When cooked remove the hearts and keep them warm. Strain the juice and then quickly reduce by half for a delicious sauce. Untie the hearts and serve with mashed swede.

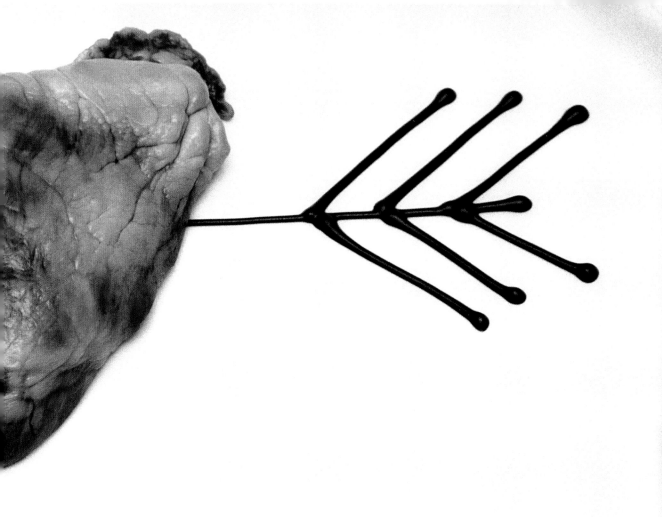

DEVILLED KIDNEYS

To serve two

6 lambs' kidneys, suet and
membrane removed, and slit
in half lengthwise, retaining
the kidney shape

3 tbsp plain flour

1 tsp cayenne pepper

1 tsp dry English mustard

sea salt and black pepper

a big knob of butter

Worcestershire sauce

a healthy splash of chicken stock

2 pieces of toast (white or brown,
up to you, though – just an
observation – white seems
to sup up the juices better)

The perfect breakfast on your birthday, with a glass of Black Velvet.

Nip out the white fatty gristle of the kidneys with a knife or scissors. Mix together the flour, cayenne pepper, mustard, and salt and pepper in a bowl.

Get a frying pan very hot, throw in a knob of butter, and as this melts roll your kidneys in your spiced flour, then shake them in a sieve to remove excess. Place them in the sizzling pan, cook for 2 minutes each side, add a hearty splash of Worcestershire sauce and the chicken stock, and let all the ingredients get to know each other. Remove the kidneys to your two waiting bits of toast, let the sauce reduce and emulsify in the pan (do not let it disappear) and pour over the kidneys and toast. Eat – Happy Birthday!

LAMB'S KIDNEYS IN THEIR SUET

To serve one

2 lamb's kidneys
the merest gesture of oil
sea salt and black pepper

Lamb's kidneys still in their suet should not be a problem for your butcher to arrange. If there are large amounts of suet, trim it down but try not to expose the actual kidney. I think two kidneys per person.

Get an ovenproof frying pan very hot, add oil, and season your kidneys thoroughly, especially with salt. Place them in the pan, brown them all over, and place the whole thing in a hot oven for 8 minutes.

Remove the kidneys from the oven and from the pan, which should be quite full of fat by now, leave them to rest somewhere warm for 4–5 minutes, then slice each one into four. You should have the salty, crispy outside of the suet, melting rich fat within, and finally in the middle, the beautiful, blushing kidney. Serve hot with a watercress salad.

MUTTON AND BEANS

To serve six happily

500g *dried borlotti beans, soaked*
overnight and drained – they have
a certain nuttiness

1 leg of mutton

butter

1.25kg piece of green streaky bacon,
cut into chunks, rind removed
and reserved

2 carrots, peeled and chopped

3 onions, peeled and chopped

3 leeks, cleaned and chopped

18 cloves of garlic, peeled
and left whole

a bundle of fresh herbs

4 bay leaves

sea salt and black pepper

½ bottle of red wine

1.5 litres chicken stock

Unfortunately it seems very hard to get your hands on mutton any more, which seems odd as not that long ago a mutton chop was fundamental in the British diet; almost no formal meal went by without it appearing somewhere. However, persistence and a good butcher should suffice.

Cover your borlotti beans with clean water and cook for 1½ hours. Check them, you want them cooked but not falling apart. Remove from the heat and drain, but keep the liquor.

Meanwhile season your mutton, get a frying pan hot, add a large knob of butter, and allow it to sizzle. Reduce the heat slightly and brown the leg of mutton in the pan. You want this to be a gentle buttery moment, not a ferocious burning moment.

Remove the mutton to an oven dish or deep roasting tray large enough to hold all the ingredients. Brown the bacon and bacon rind in the same frying pan then add to the mutton. Gently cook the vegetables and garlic (if the pan seems too dry add a bit more butter), and then add these to the mutton and bacon, and nestle the herb bundle in. Also add the cooked borlotti beans and bay leaves, season, and add the wine and stock. The contents of the dish, except the mutton, should be just covered; if this is not the case add some of the bean liquor.

Cover with tinfoil, place in a medium to gentle oven for 4 hours, turning the leg over every 40 minutes, and checking at about 3 hours with a knife. When it's ready, check the seasoning, cut chunks of giving mutton from the bone, and serve in deep plates with beans, vegetables, bacon and juices.

LAMB SHANKS
EBEN'S WAY
To serve four

4 rear lamb shanks (if front shanks, allow 2 per person)

20 raisins

4 cloves of garlic, peeled and each one sliced into 5

4 tbsp red wine vinegar

4 glasses of red wine

4 juniper berries

4 whole allspice

10 black peppercorns

3 bay leaves

sea salt

1 glass of port

Eben uses a leg of lamb, but it is the fatty qualities of the lamb shank I have found to be most suited to this dish.

Make 5 incisions into your lamb shanks, into each of which press a raisin and a slice of garlic. In a plastic or china container place the lamb shanks and all the other ingredients except the salt and port. Marinate for at least 2 days (they will not be covered – do not worry), turning the shanks every half-day or so.

You will need a heavy pan with a well-fitting lid (not aluminium, because of the vinegar). Place the shanks and marinade in it, adding a healthy pinch of salt. Cover and place in a medium to gentle oven, and cook for approximately 3 hours, turning the shanks every 30 minutes. If they are cooking too fast, turn the oven down: the secret is slow and low with this dish. The shanks want to be thoroughly giving, but still just holding on to the bone. When this is achieved, remove the shanks and keep warm. Add the glass of port to the juice, place it on the heat, and reduce until your sauce is to your satisfaction. Pour it over the shanks through a sieve (to remove the spices) and serve.

This dish goes very well with quince cheese, a conserve you can get from delicatessens, village fêtes and some supermarkets.

LAMB AND BARLEY STEW

To serve eight

2.5kg neck of lamb – shoulder and neck chops are appropriate; keep them on the bone and ask your butcher to chop them into appropriate pieces

a bundle made of thyme, parsley, and 2 sticks of celery

3 bay leaves

10 black peppercorns

sea salt

8 small carrots, peeled, or 2 big carrots, peeled and chopped in half

16 shallots, peeled

4 kohlrabies, peeled and cut in half

8 leeks, cleaned and trimmed

a good handful (or small cup) of barley; this may not seem much but it expands and has a habit of taking over

A dish which likes to be made a day before eating.

Place the lamb, herb bundle, bay leaves, peppercorns and a pinch of salt in a pan, cover with water, bring to the boil, skim, reduce to the gentlest of simmers, and add the vegetables and barley. Cook for 1 hour. Check the meat with a knife to see if it is giving, but catch it before it is overcooked (watch that it never cooks too fast). Decant into a clean china container and allow to cool in its broth.

When cold a layer of fat should form on the surface; remove this. When it comes to the eating return the lamb, vegetables, barley and broth to a pan, bring up to the boil, and reduce to a simmer until all is hot. Check the seasoning and remove the thyme bundle. Serve on deepish plates so the broth can be enjoyed as well.

Some may be tempted to add more *oomph* to this dish, but I'm all for its soothing, gentle qualities.

BRAISED SHOULDER OF LAMB

To serve four, possibly five

20 *shallots, peeled and left whole*

20 *cloves of garlic, peeled and left whole*

a splash of extra virgin olive oil

a bundle of thyme and rosemary

1 shoulder of lamb, on the bone

½ bottle of white wine

1 litre light chicken stock

sea salt and black pepper

Chop, leg, best end of lamb are all splendid, but a slow-braised shoulder of lamb … aahhh! A piece of meat with a truly giving nature.

In an oven tray deep and wide enough to house your shoulder of lamb, brown the shallots and garlic in oil. Lay the bundle of herbs in the pan and put the shoulder of lamb on top. Pour on the white wine and stock. Season the shoulder liberally.

Cover with foil and place in a gentle oven for 3-ish hours, as always keeping an eye on it and poking it with a small, sharp knife to check if it's done. As far as cooking meat goes, shoulder of lamb is one of the best-behaved joints and you don't even have to know how to carve. It is a case of attack.

KID AND FENNEL
Quantities for three

a splash of extra virgin olive oil

1 leg of kid

3 bulbs of fennel, cut against the grain into 1cm slices

12 shallots, peeled and left whole

12 cloves of garlic, peeled and left whole

a bundle of thyme, rosemary and parsley (herbs you can imagine the young kid skipping through)

sea salt and black pepper

1 small glass of Pernod

1 large glass of white wine

600ml chicken stock

a splash of extra virgin olive oil

One hind leg of kid will vary in size and can feed from two to three to sometimes four. I have to leave you to judge your leg and your appetite.

In a heated frying pan drop a splash of olive oil and brown the leg of kid, then place it in an oven dish or roasting tray. Sweat the vegetables and garlic in the pan (do not colour them) then place these around the leg of kid, add the herb bundle, seasoning, Pernod, wine, chicken stock and a splash of extra virgin olive oil – the liquid does not have to cover everything.

Cover with tinfoil and place in a hot oven for 20 minutes then turn down to medium for approximately another 2 hours; halfway through turn your leg over. Check with a knife that the leg and vegetables are cooked; if they're ready, slice the leg, and with a slotted spoon put the vegetables in a bowl. Pour the remaining juice into a jug and serve all three together.

BIRDS AND GAME

ROAST PIGEON AND OTHER GAME BIRDS
PIGEON, CHICKPEAS AND SPRING ONION
ROAST WOODCOCK
ROAST QUAIL
GIBLET STEW
DUCKS' LEGS AND CARROTS
SALTED DUCKS' LEGS, GREEN BEANS AND CORNMEAL DUMPLINGS
POACHED SALTED DUCKS' LEGS
BOILED CHICKEN, LEEKS AND AÏOLI
CHICKEN AND PIG'S TROTTER
PHEASANT AND PIG'S TROTTER PIE WITH SUET CRUST
RABBIT WRAPPED IN FENNEL TWIGS AND BACON
SADDLE OF RABBIT
RABBIT AND GARLIC
RABBIT WITH PEA AND BROAD BEAN PURÉE
JELLIED RABBIT
CONFIT OF RABBIT LEG IN BROTH
JUGGED HARE
ANOTHER THEORY OF JUGGED HARE
BRAISED FRONT LEG AND SHOULDER OF VENISON
VENISON LIVER

ROAST PIGEON AND OTHER GAME BIRDS

Allow one pigeon per person

sea salt and black pepper

2 knobs of butter and a sprig of sage per pigeon

Pigeons are wonderful when cooked properly. Maybe they're not quite as delicious as more glamorous game birds, grouse, grey leg partridge or woodcock, but they're much cheaper and available almost all the year round. Do not be put off by the urban pigeon, think woods, countryside and plump, cooing pigeons in trees.

Season the pigeons inside and out. Stick the sage into the cavity of the pigeon, with a walnut-sized knob of butter. Get an ovenproof frying pan hot, and melt some butter; when sizzling, brown your pigeon in the pan, being careful not to leave the pigeon breast down against the hot pan for too long, as this is the most delicate part.

Right your pigeon so it's breast up and place in a very hot oven for 8–10 minutes. When the butter inside the pigeon has melted it's a good indication that it's ready. Remove from the oven and place upside down on a warm plate somewhere warm but not so hot as to carry on cooking the bird (this allows the butter to seep into the breasts, and moisten them), and leave to rest for 10 minutes, by which time the breasts will be a blushing red.

Peas and pea leaves make a happy pillow for the pigeon to come and rest on. Pigeon starts with a P and so does Peas, maybe this is why they get on so well together.

Serve the pigeon with a sharp knife.

OTHER GAME BIRDS
As for other game birds, I would apply the same cooking principle, allowing a couple more minutes for larger birds. The exceptions are your partridge, which should have the faintest of blushing breasts, unlike the darker-fleshed birds and the woodcock.

PIGEON, CHICKPEAS AND SPRING ONION

To serve four

500g dried chickpeas, soaked overnight and drained

1 whole head of garlic

1 tbsp tahini

4 cloves of garlic, peeled

juice of 1 lemon

300ml extra virgin olive oil

a splash of Tabasco to taste

sea salt and black pepper

4 wood pigeons

2 bunches of spring onions, washed and trimmed

This is not really a recipe, more of a suggestion to bring together three basic, but very suited, textures and flavours.

Place your chickpeas in fresh clean water with the whole garlic and bring to the boil, then simmer for approximately 2 hours, until cooked. Drain (keep the chickpea water, as it makes a very good vegetarian stock), put half the cooked chickpeas into a food processor with the tahini and peeled garlic, whizz, and add the lemon juice and some of the oil: you are looking for a looseish consistency, not a thick glump. Add the Tabasco, salt and pepper, and the rest of the chickpeas then whizz again, but keeping these coarser – coarse is good here.

Roast the pigeons as on the previous page, allow them to cool to a warm and handleable temperature, then with a sharp knife remove the breasts and legs by following the bird's back- and breastbones down its carcass.

Serve with the chickpea purée still slightly warm and a bowl of spring onions. You have got the gamey meat, the soothing, nutty chickpea and the stimulating *gnya* of the spring onions.

ROAST WOODCOCK

Woodcock defecate before they fly, so they can be roasted with the guts in, which heightens the flavour.

Allow the same roasting and resting time as the pigeon (see page 174), then, with a teaspoon, scoop out its guts into a hot frying pan with a knob of butter, allow to sizzle for a few moments, then rescue the liver with a spoon and mix with a splash of stock, using the back of a spoon to work the ingredients together.

Rest your woodcock on a piece of toast, onto which you have spread its liver, and pour the pan juices through a sieve over the bird. The head you also roast, wrapped in tinfoil, and split open when serving, exposing its delicious brains: you will need a teaspoon for this. Unfortunately woodcock are not as plentiful as pigeons and are much more expensive, but they are worth it. They are one of the finest eating experiences.

ROAST QUAIL

To serve four

sea salt and black pepper

10 quails (as there are always those who end up eating 3)

extra virgin olive oil

The quail unfortunately falls into a kind of bird purgatory; it is not a game bird, though some describe it as such, but is now a thoroughly farmed bird, so not glamorous enough to warrant the 'hands on' battling that people feel justified to exert on grouse and partridge, and is denied from joining the chicken's gang as it is seen to be too fiddly to eat. Then finally, to kick it while the quail's down, people say it has no flavour.

Put all this behind you and let me put forward the case for the joys of a bowl of thoroughly roasted quails.

Season the quails inside and out very thoroughly, being especially heavy on the salt. In a hot frying pan, with a small splash of olive oil, brown the quails all over. When you are satisfied with their colour place them onto a lightly oiled roasting tray and put in a hot oven for 20 minutes or so.

Despite the quail's fragile reputation it is robust when it comes to cooking, not having the drying-out potential of the partridge or the angst of getting that perfect moment of blush in a grouse breast. The quail wants plenty of cooking, to the point that its legs can be pulled easily from the ribcage and the flesh sucked off the leg bone. Salty and well done, serve the quail in a bowl in the middle of the table and encourage some hands-on eating.

Serve with a bowl of lentils or simply a watercress salad.

178

GIBLET STEW

To feed six

200g white haricot beans
(this is enough for the beans
to be emphatically present,
yet the dish is not too beany),
soaked overnight and drained

2 whole heads of garlic, cut in half

6 ducks' necks, preserved in
duck fat (see page 270)

6 ducks' hearts, preserved in
duck fat

6 ducks' gizzards (once trimmed
become 2 halves), preserved
in duck fat

12 chicken wings

3 shallots, peeled and thinly sliced

2 leeks, cleaned and thinly sliced

2.5 litres duck stock or good
flavoursome chicken stock

6 slices of fresh foie gras (this may
be hard to find, but is well worth
the hunt; however, do not be
disheartened if it is unobtainable,
the dish is still delicious without)

sea salt and black pepper

When on the menu at St. John this dish's name has been known to cause some small surprise amongst our diners, but when tried it has won round the most sceptical, for it is simply wonderful.

Place the beans in a pan with the garlic. Cover with clean water, bring to the boil, skim, reduce to a simmer, and cook for approximately 2½ hours so the beans are thoroughly cooked but not falling apart. Once cooked, remove from the heat but keep in their water.

Bring your preserved giblets out of the fridge so that the fat warms up, making it easy to scrape it off. Take a pot large enough for all your ingredients, drop in a spot of duck fat, place it on the heat, and when hot, brown the chicken wings. When these are a satisfactory colour, remove from the pot and keep to one side. Now, in the same fat, sweat the shallots and leeks until soft but not burnt, return the chicken wings to the pot, add the stock and drained beans, bring to the boil, skim, and reduce to a simmer. When the chicken wings are thoroughly cooked but not falling apart, add the necks, hearts and gizzards. When these are hot through, the dish is ready; it should be loose and brothy, not thick and stewy. Season to taste.

Just before serving, float the slices of foie gras on top of the stew, the heat from which will start to melt it. Serve in deep bowls and eat with plenty of crusty white bread.

DUCKS' LEGS
AND CARROTS

To serve six

duck fat or butter

6 ducks' legs (available without the rest of the duck from most butchers)

1 white onion, peeled and sliced

2 leeks, cleaned and sliced

8 cloves of garlic, peeled and kept whole

14 medium-sized carrots, peeled and chopped into 7mm rounds

a bundle of parsley and 4 sprigs of rosemary (you have to be very careful with rosemary, since delicious as it is, it can take over)

2 bay leaves

1 chilli, kept whole

sea salt and black pepper

about 1.5 litres chicken stock

Whenever someone said they'd cooked something out of my book, it was ducks' legs and carrots.

Get a frying pan hot, add a spoonful of duck fat or butter, wait until it is sizzling, and then brown the ducks' legs on both sides. Remove from the pan and set aside. In the same pan cook the onion, leeks and garlic. Mix in the carrots and cook for 3 more minutes, then decant all the vegetables into a deep oven dish.

Nestle in the herb bundle, bay leaves and chilli (this just emits a slight warmth to the dish, unlike a more pungent chopped chilli). Press the ducks' legs into the carrot bed, skin side upwards, season the dish, and pour chicken stock over until the ducks' legs are showing like alligators in a swamp. Place into a medium to hot oven for 1½ hours, keeping an eye on it so it does not burn – if it threatens to, cover the dish with foil. Check the legs with a knife; you want them thoroughly giving.

When cooked the carrots will have drawn up the duck fat, the stock reduced to a rich juice, and the duck skin should be brown and crispy. Serve with bread to mop up the juices and follow with a green salad.

SALTED DUCKS' LEGS, GREEN BEANS AND CORNMEAL DUMPLINGS

To serve six

6 ducks' legs, which you have kept in a brine (see page 269) for a week, rinsed

1 whole garlic bulb

2 whole carrots, peeled

2 leeks, cleaned

2 sticks of celery

2 onions, peeled and halved

2 bay leaves

a bundle of fresh herbs

12 black peppercorns

1kg French beans, topped and tailed

DUMPLINGS

200g finely diced wholemeal bread

2 eggs

2 tbsp duck fat

60g minced smoked bacon

60g finely grated fresh horseradish

90g polenta

sea salt and black pepper

The dumplings are made with a recipe of Stephanie Alexander's and are so splendid I cannot improve on them in any way. I hope she does not mind me using it, but they are ideal companions to the salted duck's leg.

Cook your ducks' legs as in Poached Salted Ducks' Legs (see opposite) and while they're simmering combine all the dumpling ingredients together into a sticky mixture; it should not be dry. Roll the mixture into 2cm balls; you should have 12 dumplings.

Fifteen minutes before the ducks' legs are ready, ladle out some of the cooking liquor into another pan. Bring it to a gentle simmer and cook your dumplings in this. When the ducks' legs are ready, remove from the liquor and keep warm and moist. Strain the liquor, then return it to the pan. Bring to a rolling boil and cook the beans for 3–4 minutes.

Serve in a deep plate or shallow dish, with the beans at the bottom, and the ducks' legs and dumplings on top. Pour over a ladle of liquor and eat.

POACHED SALTED DUCKS' LEGS

To serve six

6 ducks' legs, which you have kept
in a brine (see page 269) for a
week, rinsed

1 whole garlic bulb

2 whole carrots, peeled

2 leeks, cleaned

2 sticks of celery

2 onions, peeled and halved

2 bay leaves

a bundle of fresh herbs

12 black peppercorns

This is a dish you have to think about a week ahead.

Place the ducks' legs in a pan with all the other ingredients. Cover with clean water, bring gently to the boil, then reduce to a calm simmer for approximately 1 hour: you want them giving but not completely falling from the bone. Serve with lentils, as with Boiled Belly (see page 114).

BOILED CHICKEN, LEEKS AND AÏOLI

Feeds three easily

1 free-range chicken (slit the skin between the leg and breast)

2 carrots

2 leeks

1 onion

1 whole head of garlic

2 sticks of celery, chopped

2 bay leaves

a bundle of thyme, parsley and rosemary

black peppercorns

sea salt

Aïoli (see page 252)

8 leeks, trimmed

This may sound complicated, but it's actually quite simple and is emphatically worth it.

Place the bird and all the ingredients except the aïoli and the eight trimmed leeks in a large pot, cover with cold water, and bring to the boil. As soon as it boils cover it with a lid, take it off the heat, and leave it to cool.

Remove the chicken from the stock. Strain the stock then return it with the chicken to a clean pot, retaining enough of the broth for another pot for your leeks. Bring the stock up to a gentle simmer. Allow the immersed chicken to heat through thoroughly for 30 minutes; you will now have a moist bird that is not falling apart or toughened from hard boiling. Bring the stock for the leeks to the boil, drop them in, and cook them for about 8–10 minutes, depending on their size.

Serve the chicken and leeks with a splash of the chicken broth, a bowl of the aïoli, and coarse sea salt. As with any boiled unbrined meat, coarse sea salt applied just before eating is very good. Save the rest of the stock for future cooking.

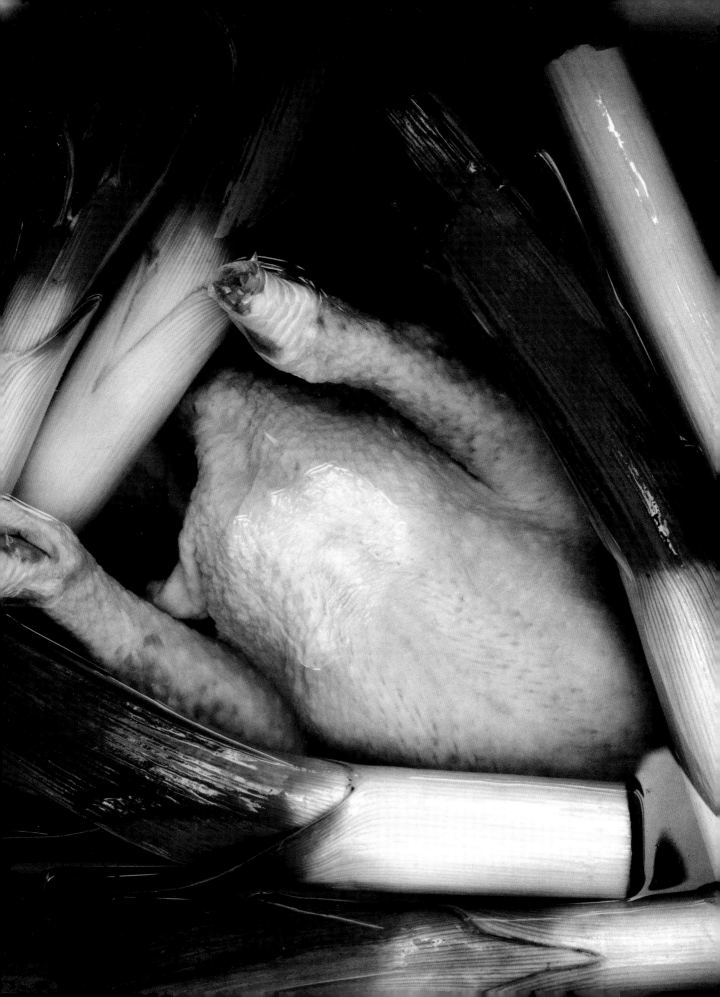

CHICKEN AND PIG'S TROTTER

To serve four

3 pig's trotters

2 carrots, peeled

1 whole head of garlic

2 onions, peeled and halved

a bundle of fresh herbs

2 bay leaves

2 sticks of celery, chopped

1 leek, cleaned

12 black peppercorns

1 bottle of red wine

2 litres chicken stock

duck fat or butter

450g piece of smoked streaky bacon, the rind removed in one piece, rolled and tied, and the bacon cut into chunks

12 shallots, peeled

1 chicken, jointed and seasoned

sea salt and black pepper

Chicken with a trotter force field.

In a pan place the trotters, carrots, garlic, onions, herb bundle, bay leaves, celery, leek and peppercorns, cover with wine and chicken stock, cover with the lid, and place in a medium oven for 3 hours until the trotters are thoroughly cooked. Remove the trotters from the pan and allow to cool until handleable. Strain the remaining liquor into a clean pan, discard the vegetables, and place on the heat. Bring to a simmer and allow to reduce.

Meanwhile your trotters have cooled, so pluck the skin and flesh off the bones and add this to your simmering sauce, and cook for 1 hour. Then get a frying pan hot, add duck fat or butter and brown the bacon and shallots, and add these to your simmering pot (do not clean the frying pan); let this all cook together for a further 30 minutes.

Meanwhile, in the frying pan you have kept, brown your pieces of chicken. Place the chicken in an oven dish, then pour over it the trotter, bacon and shallot mixture and the juice. Check for seasoning as the bacon will give saltiness. Cover and place in a hot oven for 40 minutes, then uncover for 10 minutes more.

When it's ready, serve straight away with mashed potato. A delicious extra for dipping in the sauce is triangles of white bread fried in duck fat.

PHEASANT AND PIG'S TROTTER PIE WITH SUET CRUST

A pie for six

This is a most rich and steadying pie.

The pie filling is best made the day before, to find itself. Place the trotters in a pan with the herbs, garlic, bay leaves, peppercorns, celery, red onions and carrots, cover with red wine and stock, bring to the boil, then reduce to a simmer for 3 hours until the trotters are cooked and tender. Remove the trotters from the pan then strain the stock. While the trotters are warm pick the flesh and skin from the bones.

Get a frying pan hot, add duck fat or butter, fry the bacon chunks and the rolled skin, then remove to a deep roasting tray or oven dish. Now brown the pheasant halves, and then move them to join the bacon (if the pan is looking dry add a little more fat). Then sweat the onions, add these to the roasting tray, add the trotter flesh and stock, and cover with tinfoil. Place in a hot oven for 15 minutes, then reduce the heat to medium and cook for another 30 minutes. Remove, check the seasoning and allow to cool in the stock (at this point it can be eaten if you have not the patience for making a pie).

When cool remove the pheasant and pull the meat off the bones, keeping the pieces of flesh large as you want them to maintain their integrity in the pie. Return them to the other ingredients and refrigerate overnight.

To make the pastry, mix all the ingredients except the egg yolk together, then add cold water cautiously to achieve a firm dough. Allow this to rest in the fridge for at least 2 hours before use.

Place your mixture in a pie dish (if there appears to be too much sauce, hold some back, it will come in handy somewhere else), cover with pastry, paint this with egg yolk, and bake in a medium to hot oven for 40 minutes. When the pastry is ready and golden, and the stuffing bubbling inside, serve and eat. Very good with Brussels sprouts.

RABBIT WRAPPED IN FENNEL TWIGS AND BACON

PER WHOLE RABBIT

a healthy splash of extra virgin olive oil

sea salt and black pepper

a bundle of dried fennel twigs (obtained from good food shops, or you can pick/dry them yourself)

20 slices of smoked streaky bacon

4 whole heads of garlic

¼ bottle of white wine

500ml chicken stock

This dish can be made with wild or tame rabbits. The pros and cons are as follows. With the wild, you need a good source as they are often badly shot up or mauled by ferrets, which tends to leave them as an off-putting mess of blood clots. (What you need is a good shot, who can get them in the head.) Though somewhat tougher, they have much more flavour than tame rabbit, which can sometimes be almost too subtle (though this can vary according to where the rabbits come from: Norfolk wild rabbits seem to have an easier time, which is reflected in their flesh, compared, say, to a Welsh rabbit, the angst in whose life seems to be apparent in the eating – though this is particularly suited to some dishes). Tame are much larger and meatier, and should be more constant, and of course do not suffer from the same wounds as the wild.

A tame rabbit will certainly feed four. A wild rabbit will feed between two or three, depending on its size.

Splash and rub your rabbit with oil, season enthusiastically, then surround with dried fennel twigs from end to end and tummy to back (so it starts to look like a scene from *The Wicker Man*). Hold these in place by wrapping the whole thing in the strips of streaky bacon.

Lay in a deepish roasting tray or dish, nestle garlic next to the rabbit, pour wine and stock around it, and roast in a medium to hot oven for approximately 1½ hours, depending on the size of the rabbit (tame ones may only take 1 hour); stab its thigh to see if it is giving. The aim of this dish is a rabbit that's well cooked, but still moist thanks to the insulation we have provided.

When cooked remove the twigs. Unfortunately they are not edible, but the bacon should be wonderfully crispy. With a cleaver or heavy knife, chop the rabbit into chunks and serve with the garlic and a jug of the juice.

SADDLE OF RABBIT

To serve four

4 tame or 6 wild rabbit saddles, with their kidneys

sea salt and black pepper

500g thinly sliced green streaky bacon or back fat

a bundle of caul fat (your butcher should have no problem obtaining this for you)

extra virgin olive oil

Vinaigrette (see page 253)

From a good butcher you should be able to obtain just the saddles of rabbit; if not, you can always use the legs for something else (try Confit, page 194). You will need a tame rabbit or a particularly happy wild rabbit for this dish. Take the fillets off the bone (2 per portion if tame, 3 if wild) with a thin sharp knife, following the backbone and ribs, or ask your butcher. Remove the kidneys and save them.

Roughly chop the kidneys. Lay out 4 tame or 6 wild fillets, on which you apply the chopped kidneys. Season, then sandwich with the remaining fillets. Roll these in streaky bacon and then in a thin layer of caul fat to hold them together, to produce a kind of rabbit and bacon cigar.

Get an ovenproof frying pan hot, apply a spot of oil, and let this heat up. Then brown your rabbit rolls thoroughly (this is very important as you want to crisp up and cook away the caul fat, so you do not end up with a stringy, chewy, fatty outside). When a pleasing brown, place the frying pan into a hot oven for 10–12 minutes. You want to catch the flesh just as it loses its pink translucent quality.

Serve it with a salad that captures the spirit of Mr McGregor's garden, made up from, for example, spring onions, baby carrots, radishes, peas and broad beans, if in season, rocket and chopped parsley (a subliminal caper if you feel so inclined – I do!). Dress with vinaigrette and eat with the succulent rabbit.

RABBIT AND GARLIC

To serve ten

2 healthy splashes of extra
virgin olive oil

2 tame rabbits, chopped into
sections (if you don't have a cleaver
or a heavy knife, ask your butcher)

sea salt and black pepper

300g smoked streaky bacon,
cut into spirited chunks and
rind reserved

24 shallots, peeled but kept whole

60–80 cloves of garlic, unpeeled

300ml dry sherry

600ml white wine

1 litre chicken stock

2 bay leaves

a bundle of thyme and parsley
tied together

There was a wonderful rabbit I ate in Barcelona, which was dry but wet, salty but not too salty, and above all garlicky. This recipe came out of attempting to recreate it. In fact, except for the garlic it is nothing like it, but still delicious none the less.

Get a large ovenproof pot with a lid, place on the heat, and pour in enough olive oil to just cover the bottom. Season the rabbit pieces with salt and pepper and when the oil is hot brown the rabbit. When you are happy with the hue, remove them from the pot (if all the oil has gone with them add another splash). Put in the bacon, its skin and the shallots, allow to sizzle, and stir for 10 minutes, not letting them burn. Now return the rabbit to the pot and add the garlic, sherry, wine, stock, bay leaves, and finally the bundle of thyme and parsley. Check the seasoning. Bring to a boil, straight away reduce to a simmer, place the lid on and put the pot into a warm to hot oven for approximately 1½ hours, but keep an eye on it and check the meat for giving qualities with a sharp knife (not quite but soon to fall off the bone).

Serve hot straight from the pot, encouraging your fellow diners to suck the flesh from the unpeeled garlic cloves, which will now be sweet and delicious. For the juices you will need both bread and napkins.

RABBIT WITH PEA AND BROAD BEAN PURÉE

To serve four

extra virgin olive oil

1 tame rabbit, jointed
and seasoned

2 leeks, cleaned and chopped

1 good-sized potato, peeled
and chopped

1 onion, peeled and chopped

1.5 litres chicken stock

2 cloves of garlic, peeled
and chopped

a bundle of thyme and parsley

sea salt and black pepper

1kg fresh peas in pod, podded

1kg fresh broad beans
in pod, podded

sea salt and black pepper

Vinaigrette (see page 253)

a handful of fresh mint, picked
and chopped just before using

This dish lends itself to the gentler flesh of tame rabbit, rather than wild. You could substitute chicken.

Take a pot large enough to fit all the ingredients, add a splash of olive oil, and get it hot. Lightly brown your pieces of rabbit, then remove; then add the leeks, potato and onion. Sweat these – not too much colouring – and return the rabbit to the pan. Cover it with stock and add the garlic and herbs. Check the seasoning and bring it gently to the boil, then reduce to a very gentle simmer for 40 minutes. Remove the rabbit, moisten it with a splash of juice, and keep it warm. Bring the stock and vegetables back to the boil, add the peas and beans, and boil for 5 minutes, until they are cooked but not mushy and losing their colour. Now strain the contents of your pot, keeping the juice (this will make wonderful soup) and the vegetables separate. Place the vegetables in a food processor and purée (if they are too dry add some of the juice).

Check the seasoning and mix the mint with the vinaigrette.

Serve the purée with the rabbit, over which you pour some of the vinaigrette, and accompany it with hot beetroot. The combination of colours looks very fine and it tastes fantastic.

JELLIED RABBIT

To serve four

1 tame rabbit or 2 wild rabbits,
chopped up but bone in – if tame,
you may get 3 sections out
of the saddle

10 shallots, peeled and finely sliced

1 bottle of white wine

2 pig's trotters

2 whole heads of garlic

a bundle of thyme

10 black peppercorns

1 litre light chicken stock

400g thinly sliced green
streaky bacon

2 bay leaves

sea salt and black pepper

Use tame or particularly beautiful wild rabbits for this. Be warned, this takes about two days to prepare.

Marinate the rabbit and shallots in the white wine in a non-metal container in the fridge overnight. Meanwhile place the trotters in a pan with the garlic, thyme and peppercorns, cover with the chicken stock, and bring them to a gentle simmer. Cover and, keeping an eye on it, cook for 3 hours. Strain (if you want to you can add the trotter flesh to the final dish, otherwise discard it), return to a pan, and reduce by half. Allow to cool.

Next day, line an ovenproof crock with the bacon. Mix the rabbit and marinade with the trotter stock (this may have jellied so it might have to be melted) and bay leaves. Check the seasoning, remembering the salty bacon factor, and also that you will be eating it cold so it will need a flavour boost. Pour the rabbit and its mixture into the lined crock, cover, and place in a medium oven for 2½ hours, keeping an eye on it so it never cooks too fast. Check with a small sharp knife that the rabbits are cooked. When cooked allow the whole crock to cool and then place it in the fridge overnight. Next day serve cold from the crock with hot boiled potatoes, with lots of chopped curly parsley.

CONFIT OF RABBIT LEG IN BROTH
To serve four

4 rabbit hind legs

12 shallots, peeled but whole

12 small turnips (if possible with greens, cut off but kept)

12 baby carrots, trim off greens

sea salt and black pepper

Aïoli (see page 252)

This is an excellent way of using your rabbit legs after making the boned Saddle of Rabbit on page 190. They will need to be turned into confit first, though.

Make a stock with the rabbit bones (see Stocks, page 264). If there are not enough, add chicken bones.

Confit your rabbit using the method on page 270. If you have some ready, so much the better, get it out of the fridge so that it comes to kitchen temperature and it's easy to wipe most of the fat off with your fingers.

Bring your stock to the boil and add the shallots. Cook for 10 minutes then add the rest of the vegetables, except the turnip greens. Cook for another 8 minutes then reduce the broth to a gentle simmer. Add the rabbit legs and let them gently heat through and soften. When they are ready and the vegetables are cooked, add the turnip greens and allow them to wilt; season to taste. Serve in deep plates or shallow bowls so a ladle of broth can be poured over each serving. Eat with aïoli.

JUGGED HARE

To serve four

450g plain flour

1 tsp crushed mace

1 tsp crushed cloves

1 tsp crushed allspice

sea salt and black pepper

1 hare, gutted and jointed, any blood reserved and mixed with a small splash of red wine vinegar

2 tsp butter

3 red onions, peeled and chopped

3 carrots, peeled and chopped

3 sticks of celery, chopped

2 leeks, cleaned and chopped

½ bottle of red wine

a bundle of fresh herbs

2 cloves of garlic, peeled

2 bay leaves

2 litres chicken stock

1 large glass of port

The hare's blood is vital for this dish, so if you are not gutting the beast yourself, ask your butcher to make sure they reserve any blood. It is important to mix a small splash of red wine vinegar into the blood as soon as possible to prevent it curdling, something I am sure the butcher will do for you if you are not there at the moment of gutting and chopping.

Mix together the flour, mace, cloves, allspice, and salt and pepper, and roll your pieces of hare in this. At the same time heat the butter in a large pan. Brown the floured hare gently in the pan (it is important to do this just as the hare has been floured as otherwise the flour coating will go damp and sticky and *globdulate*). When brown, remove the hare and add the vegetables to the pan. Cook to achieve a nice colour, but not burnt. Return the hare to the pan with the wine, herbs, garlic and bay leaves, season cautiously, cover with chicken stock, cover, and place in a low to medium oven for 3 hours.

When cooked, remove the hare from the mixture and strain the liquor. Discard the vegetables. You can prepare the dish ahead up to this point. Return the hare to the sauce, allow it to cool, and set it aside, preferably in the fridge unless you are eating it the same day. To serve, return the sauce to the heat, add the port, and boil quickly for 5 minutes. Reduce the heat so the sauce is not boiling (very important), stir in the blood, and allow the sauce to thicken. Return the hare to the sauce and serve with mashed potato.

ANOTHER THEORY
OF JUGGED HARE

For this you will need two hares to feed four

This entails two days of eating hare. On the first day you have the saddle and you jug the legs as before, but keep them for the next day.

THE FIRST DAY

Remove the back and front legs and shoulders as for Jugged Hare (see opposite), but keep the saddles whole. My feeling is that the legs lend themselves perfectly to jugging, but the leaner saddle has a habit of drying out. So to do them justice, fillet the saddles (just follow the bones with a sharp knife), season, get an ovenproof frying pan very hot, add butter, and allow it to sizzle. Seal the fillets in the pan and place in a hot oven for 4 minutes. Remove the fillets to a warm plate, put them in a warm place, and allow them to rest for 10 minutes. Serve with delicious, rich Mashed Parsnips (see page 244). This is wonderful.

THE SECOND DAY

Reheat the legs gently in a pan with the lid on in a medium oven and follow with the port and blood procedure described in Jugged Hare. This may seem like a lot of hare for one weekend, but I feel it does more justice to the various bits of the animal.

BRAISED FRONT LEG AND SHOULDER OF VENISON

To feed approximately eight

duck fat or butter

450g green streaky bacon, cut into chunks, skin off in one piece

6 carrots, peeled and chopped

6 leeks, cleaned and chopped

4 onions, peeled and sliced

400g dried ceps (just imagine the deer running through the woods, trampling wild mushrooms) soaked in 575ml hot water for 2 hours

1 front leg and shoulder of venison

12 whole cloves of garlic, peeled

a bundle of fresh herbs

sea salt and black pepper

1 bottle of red wine

1 litre chicken stock

Before you embark on this, make sure you have a roasting tray large enough for one leg and whole shoulder of venison. You can, if you need to, cut the leg at the joint, to make it fit.

Place your roasting tray onto the heat, melt the duck fat or butter, and sweat the bacon, bacon skin and vegetables until they soften. Add the drained ceps (reserving the mushroom water), cook for another 4 minutes, then nestle in the venison, garlic and herbs. Season, add the wine, stock and mushroom water, cover with tinfoil, and place in a medium oven for approximately 3–3½ hours.

Because of the cartilage and fat at this end of the animal, the meat should not dry out as venison is prone to do but remain tender, and even *unctuous*. Serve with its accompanying vegetables and juices, and mashed potato.

VENISON LIVER

Venison offal is a joy. For some reason I imagined it would taste dark, bitter and of iron – how wrong could I have been? Venison liver is sweet, delicate and tender. I have heard that their brains are fantastic, but are the culinary treat of the gillie.

A plea: use venison offal when you can; treat as other offal, just make sure you know for your own peace of mind where it harks from.

Venison liver goes very well with roasted beetroot, braised chicory or mash.

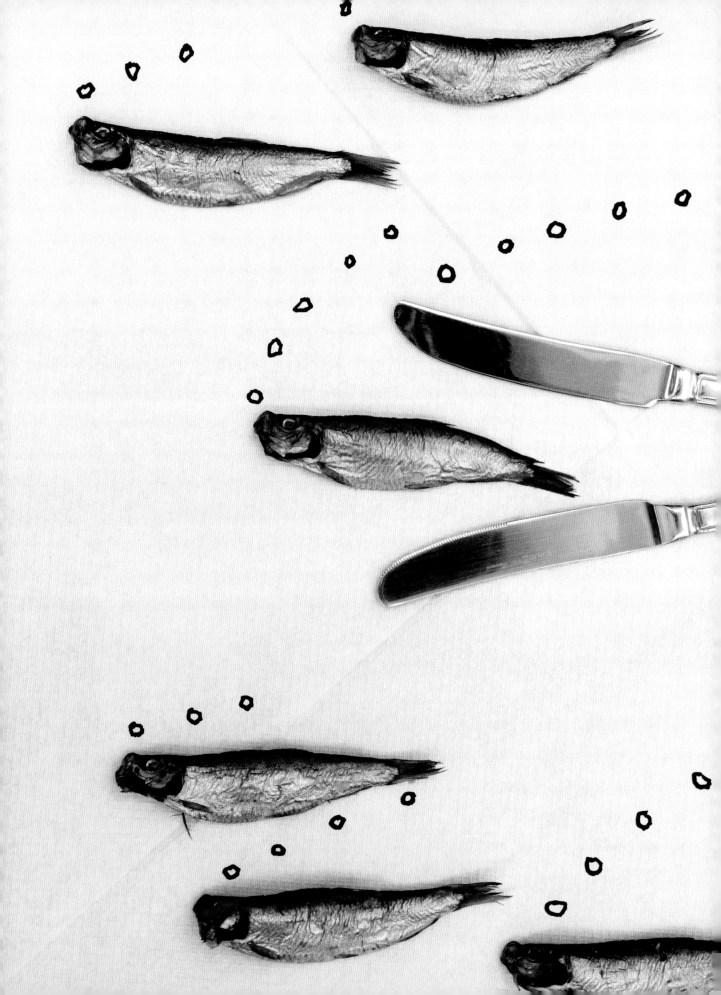

FISH AND SHELLFISH

CRAB AND MAYONNAISE

DEVILLED CRAB

KEDGEREE

FISH PIE

SMOKED HADDOCK, MUSTARD AND SAFFRON

EEL, BACON AND PRUNE STEW

SMOKED EEL, BACON AND MASH

GRILLED MUSSELS ON A BARBECUE

GRILLED MACKEREL

SALTING COD AND LING

SALT COD AND BEANS

SALT COD, POTATO AND TOMATO

SALT COD, POTATO AND GARLIC PURÉE

SKATE, CAPERS AND BREAD

HAIRY TATTIES

BRILL BAKED ON GREEN AND WHITE VEGETABLES

GREY MULLET, FENNEL TWIGS AND JERUSALEM ARTICHOKES

SOFT ROES ON TOAST

CRAB AND MAYONNAISE

This probably does not count as a recipe, more like a few thoughts.

Preferably you want to get your crabs alive. Some say you should kill them before placing them into boiling water, as this is kinder to the crab: turn them over and there is a flap; lift this to reveal a slight dip then with something like a knitting needle and hammer, spear the crab, aiming towards the front of the crab and down. I am afraid I just drop the living crab into boiling water, which must be as salty as the sea otherwise water will leach into the crab, resulting in wet flesh. Cooking time depends on the crab's size; as a rough guide, for the first 500g allow 15 minutes, then another 5 minutes per further 500g.

When it's cold remove the main shell and clean out the 'dead men's fingers', which are greyish, coarse slightly fluffy gills each side of the central body. Once this is done everything else is edible. Eat and enjoy with suitable tools to assist you in cracking open the claws and scraping out the meat from tight corners. There is almost nothing finer than a lunch spent wrestling with a crab. Keep the shells for stock.

Eat with Mayonnaise (see page 251) that is not too stiff, as this does not make a friendly partner for your crab.

DEVILLED CRAB

To feed six

3 x 1kg crabs

a healthy splash of extra virgin olive oil

4 cloves of garlic, peeled and chopped very finely

2 fresh red chillies, seeds removed and chopped very finely

100g fresh ginger, peeled and grated very finely

12 spring onions, cleaned, trimmed and chopped

juice of 2 lemons

sea salt and black pepper

half a bunch of washed picked coriander, just disciplined by the merest chopping

half a bunch of picked flat-leaf parsley, just disciplined by the merest chopping

This recipe is from Su Rogers, my best friend's mum – I beg her pardon for altering it a little, for I recall more of the meat is picked out of the shell in her recipe, whereas I enjoy the hard work at the eating moment. It is also the only dish in this book that contains coriander.

Cook and prepare the crabs as in the previous recipe; for this recipe you want to boil them for 20 minutes, on the side of under- rather than overcooked, as they are cooked again. Scoop all the meat out of the shell into a bowl and remove all the legs from the body. With a strong knife, cut the body into quarters and partially crack the large claws with a hammer.

In a pan heat the olive oil and fry the garlic, chilli and ginger for 3 minutes. Add the quartered crab bodies, the claws, the spring onion, and then the scooped crab meat and all the legs, and the lemon juice. Season and stir continuously and enthusiastically until heated through.

Just before serving, throw in the coriander and parsley, give one last stir, tip into a dish, and eat armed with useful tools to pick out the crab flesh, and many napkins, and for that matter, much white wine.

KEDGEREE

To serve six

2 sides of natural smoked haddock

much butter

400g long grain rice

sea salt

2 red onions, peeled and sliced

1 lemon

black pepper

4 hardboiled eggs, peeled
and roughly chopped

a big handful of chopped
curly parsley

My very basic kedgeree, ideal for eating morning, noon or night.

Place the haddock in a roasting tray with healthy knobs of butter and 200ml water and cook in a hot oven for 10 minutes, then remove from the oven, allow it to cool, and skin it. Save the juice in the tray and roughly flake the fish. Place the rice in a pan, lay your hand flat on the rice, and add enough water to cover your hand. Add a pinch of salt, bring to the boil, and simmer for about 20 minutes, then check the rice and drain off any excess water.

Gently fry the onions in butter in a big frying pan, so that they go soft and sweet rather than brown and burnt. Add the fish and rice and the liquor from the haddock pan, adding more butter if the mixture seems dry or is sticking (this dish is a very good vehicle for butter). When all the ingredients are heated through, squeeze the lemon onto it, season, stir in the egg and parsley, season again, and serve. It is very good by itself, but does go very well with Green Bean Chutney (see page 259).

FISH PIE
A pie for four

3 fillets natural smoked haddock

10 black peppercorns

500ml milk

150g butter

100g plain flour

sea salt and black pepper

4 x 10-minute hardboiled eggs

MASHED POTATOES

1.5kg potatoes, peeled and cut into quarters (Maris Pipers are good mashers)

300ml milk

150g butter

sea salt and black pepper

There's nothing more soothing than a fish pie.

In an ovenproof dish, cover the smoked haddock and peppercorns with the milk and bake in a medium to hot oven for approximately 20 minutes. Check the fish has cooked through; it should easily flake when prodded with a knife. Remove it from the milk, strain and save the milk, and flake the fish flesh off their skins into hearty bite-size chunks.

Meanwhile boil and mash your potatoes with the milk, butter and seasoning. While this happens, melt 100g butter in a pan, and when it's starting to bubble, add the flour and stir until the mixture smells biscuity (this suggests the flour is cooked), but do not let the mixture change colour. There must be no browning at all, so be cautious with the heat. Then add the warm fish milk, whisking (as long as it is not an aluminium pan) as you go to avoid lumps. Let the sauce thicken until it easily coats the back of your spoon and check the seasoning.

Now we are ready to construct the fish pie. In a pie dish place your haddock and hardboiled eggs. Pour over your fishy white sauce, leaving room for you to spread on the top layer of mashed potato. Then run a fork across the top of the mash, as if ploughing a field. This is not for mere decoration, but aids the crisping up factor.

Dot the top with little knobs of butter, place the pie in a hot oven, and cook for 30 minutes or until piping hot and golden brown. Serve with boiled peas.

Even just writing this recipe down, its soothing qualities have quite restored me from the fragile state in which I was.

SMOKED HADDOCK, MUSTARD AND SAFFRON

To feed four

200ml white wine

100ml water

a splash of white wine vinegar

½ tsp English mustard powder

a healthy pinch of saffron

black pepper

2 medium fillets of natural smoked haddock, cut in half fairly

a largish knob of unsalted butter

A version of a medieval dish, very yellow and delicious.

Mix together the wine, water, vinegar, mustard powder, saffron, and pepper. Place your pieces of smoked haddock into an ovenproof frying pan, pour the wine and saffron mixture over them, loosely cover with butter paper or tinfoil and place in a medium to hot oven for approximately 15 minutes, until all is piping hot.

When it is, remove from the oven, place the fish on a warm, deep plate, and put the pan of sauce onto the heat and allow to boil. Add the butter and stir briskly until the sauce and butter have emulsified. Now pour over the fish and serve hot with mashed potato.

EEL, BACON
AND PRUNE STEW

To serve eight – once you've done battle with the eels, you want to have a party

700g piece of smoked streaky bacon (rind removed in one piece, tied and rolled), cut into chunks

butter

30 whole shallots, peeled

8 cloves of garlic, peeled

1 bottle of red wine

1.1 litres light chicken stock

a bundle made of fresh herbs and 2 sticks of celery

2 bay leaves

400g prunes (Agen if possible), with their stones in (when they have been stoned they tend to fall apart in cooking, also you are left with nothing to play tinker, tailor, soldier, sailor with)

2 reasonable-sized eels (if small 3), cut into 3cm sections

a small splash of red wine vinegar

sea salt and black pepper

You can get your eels from the fishmonger in Chinatown in London, or most good fishmongers. I recall reading somewhere someone saying that skinning an eel is like removing a lady's stocking. It is not, so leave the skin on. It will do no harm, and in fact holds the flesh together and enriches the sauce. Do, though, with a good pair of scissors, trim off the fins that run along the top and bottom of the eel.

In a pot large enough to fit all your ingredients brown the bacon and its rind in butter. When the bacon has coloured and has given off some of its fat, remove and keep to one side, then gently cook the shallots and garlic in the pot to a sweet golden brown. Return the bacon and skin to the pot, then add the red wine, stock, bundle of herbs, bay leaves and prunes, and let this simmer for 15 minutes. Then add the eel and cook for a further 30 minutes.

Now carefully remove all the ingredients with a slotted spoon into a bowl, discarding the herbs, and keep warm. Add your wee dash of vinegar to the sauce to counteract the sweetness of the prunes and the richness of the eel, and bring it to a boil to reduce, skimming constantly to remove any scum that may arise. This may take 10–15 minutes.

The sauce should have a rich stickiness thanks to the eel and prunes. When happy with the juice check for seasoning and reduce the heat to a simmer. Return the other ingredients to the pot, let them warm through gently. Serve with lots of white crusty bread or mashed potato or white bread fried in duck fat. The prunes should have swollen to delicious rich clouds.

SMOKED EEL, BACON AND MASH

To feed three

1 reasonably large whole smoked eel

2kg floury potatoes (Maris Piper are good)

600ml milk

150g unsalted butter, plus an extra knob of butter for frying

sea salt and black pepper

6 thick rashers of good-quality smoked streaky bacon

More of an assemblage than a recipe as such.

To prepare your eel, first lay it down with its back facing you. With a sharp knife cut behind its head until you feel the backbone, then run your knife along the bone to the tail. Turn over and repeat. To remove the skin simply slip your fingers under it and run gently along the fillet. Cut both fillets into 3 pieces. Smoked eel is also available packaged in fillets.

Peel and halve your potatoes, and boil them until soft in salted water. Heat the milk and butter then add to the drained potatoes and mash. Season to taste, remembering that the bacon is quite salty.

Heat a frying pan and add a knob of butter. Place your bacon slices in the pan and cook. When cooked remove the bacon, keep it warm, and place the eel fillets in the pan, giving them a few moments' cooking either side in the butter and the fat the bacon should have released.

Serve the eel on a mound of mashed potato, topped with two slices of bacon, over which pour the remaining bacon and eel fat from the frying pan.

GRILLED MUSSELS ON A BARBECUE

To feed four

4kg mussels, cleaned

2 healthy handfuls of curly parsley, finely chopped

2 healthy handfuls of picked celery leaves, lightly chopped

DRESSING

juice of 2 lemons

4 cloves of garlic, finely crushed

1 tbsp young thyme leaves, chopped

400ml extra virgin olive oil

sea salt and black pepper

Ideally you are on a Hebridean island, eating mussels you have picked and cooked on driftwood. This works just as well for large clams or razor clams.

Get your barbecue to that perfect glowing moment (preferably using wood with a good history, as I am sure this helps the flavour) and simply throw your mussels on the griddle. The joy of this is they now simply cook in their own juices.

As soon as they open, scoop them up into a bowl, add the dressing, parsley and celery leaves, and toss thoroughly. Eat while hot.

GRILLED MACKEREL

This recipe has quite particular requirements but please feel free to adapt them to suit your own situation.

A driftwood fire on a beach in the Hebrides, mackerel caught that day, filleted (put knife in behind the gills, turn towards its tail, then, following the backbone, pull the knife down towards the tail; flip over and repeat on the other side). When the embers are just so, place the mackerel, skin-side down, on the griddle. By the time the skin is happy and crispy, the fillets should be cooked.

Pop into a bap with some horseradish, sit on a rock and eat with lots of white wine. 'Did anyone remember to pack the corkscrew?'

SALTING COD
AND LING
To serve four

plenty of coarse sea salt

1 cod or ling with no head or guts, split down from its stomach cavity towards its tail

Something for the future.

Open the fish up flat, this will entail some careful cutting through bones, then with a handful of salt and a tea towel gently remove any remaining blood.

In a plastic tray sprinkle a layer of salt, lay your fish on this, then cover it with salt and place it in the fridge. Check it each day and tip off any liquid and add dry salt as necessary. Once the fish is firm and has ceased to release liquid (approximately 10 days), remove from its tray, leaving the salt that has adhered to the fish attached, tie string around its tail and hang in a dry airy place. It does not have to be cold, but must not be hot. Leave until it is dry and firm; it will now keep for ages.

When you want to use it, cut off the amount you are going to cook with and soak in running water (or certainly regularly change the water) for at least 12 hours.

Of course if your fridge is not big enough for a whole cod you can do this with a cod fillet, and indeed you can buy very good salt cod.

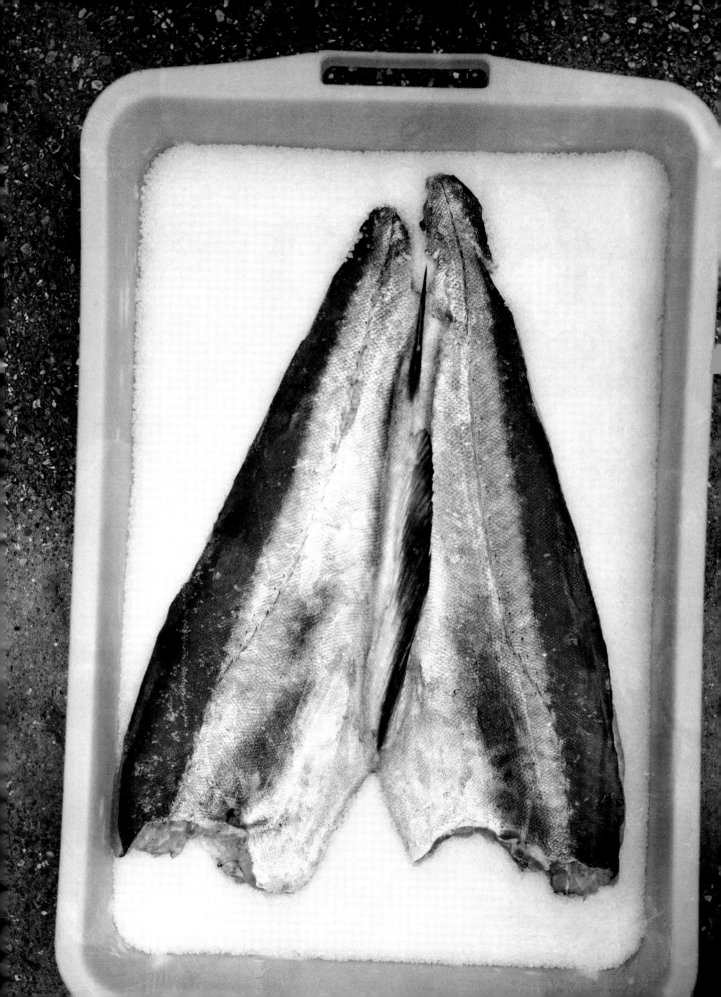

SALT COD AND BEANS

To serve six

500g *dried white haricot beans, soaked overnight*

1 whole head of garlic

2 bay leaves

2 onions, peeled and sliced

12 cloves of garlic, peeled and quartered

2 heads of fennel, sliced against the grain

extra virgin olive oil

800g *chorizo, the variety suitable for cooking (I realize this is not strictly a British sausage, but it comes under my list of ingredients that will travel), sliced into 1cm thick rounds*

½ *tin of peeled plum tomatoes*

a bundle of fresh herbs

1 litre chicken stock

sea salt and black pepper

1kg *salt cod of the lightly salted variety (see page 214), soaked overnight, cut into 6 pieces*

Fish fingers and baked beans grow up.

Drain the beans from their soaking water, cover in clean cold water in a pan, add the head of garlic and the bay leaves, bring to the boil, reduce to a simmer and cook for approximately 2 hours. When thoroughly cooked, remove from the heat and drain, keeping the bean juice.

Meanwhile in another pan sweat the onions, garlic cloves and fennel in olive oil until soft, then add the chorizo, followed very shortly by the tomatoes, crushed in your hand as you place them in the pan. Nestle in the bundle of herbs and let this mixture cook for another 20 minutes then add the beans and enough stock to just cover all the ingredients (if you do not have enough stock, use bean water). Simmer for 1 hour, allowing all the ingredients to acclimatize to each other.

Bring a pan of clean water to a gentle simmer, and when your beans are ready and you have checked them for seasoning, poach the salt cod pieces for 6–8 minutes in the water. Finally carefully lift and drain the cod, and serve on top of a mound of your beans.

SALT COD, POTATO AND TOMATO

To serve six

800g tomatoes, vine or plum are probably most appropriate, cut in half lengthwise and the green hard piece where the stem meets the tomato removed

24 cloves of garlic, peeled

sea salt and black pepper

250ml extra virgin olive oil

1.5kg good flavoursome potatoes, peeled and cut into chunks, pebbles on the beach style

1kg salt cod of the lightly salted variety (see page 214), soaked overnight then skinned and cut into 3cm chunks

a big handful of curly parsley, chopped

3 free-range hardboiled eggs, chopped

Yum.

Place your tomatoes and garlic in an oven dish, and sprinkle with salt and pepper and a healthy coating of oil. Cook in a medium oven until soft and giving (check that the garlic is cooked too; if not, remove the tomatoes to a bowl, leaving the garlic in the tomatoey oil, and return it to the oven until it is properly cooked). Hang on to the tomatoey oil.

Meanwhile cook your potatoes in gently boiling salted water. Also bring another pan of clean water to a gentle rolling simmer, which you will cook the cod in.

When the potatoes, tomatoes, and garlic are ready, poach the salt cod gently for 5 minutes. Then in a bowl bring together the drained potatoes and cod, the tomatoes and garlic with their oil, and the parsley, and season and mix gently (the cod will crumble, which is fine). Top with the egg and serve.

SALT COD, POTATO AND GARLIC PURÉE

To serve eight as a starter, or six as a main course

600g salt cod (see page 214), soaked for over 12 hours in cold water (changed as often as possible)

300g floury potatoes, peeled and cut into quarters

500ml milk

500ml extra virgin olive oil

12 whole garlic cloves, peeled

black pepper

8 free-range eggs

You need a food processor for this recipe, which is the St. John version of *brandade de morue.*

Place your salt cod into a pan of clean water and bring to the boil, then reduce to a gentle simmer for 14 minutes. Remove the fish from the water and allow to cool to a handleable heat. Remove any bones and skin (be warned – this is very sticky).

Meanwhile cook your potatoes in salted water, as if for mashing. Drain when done. In two separate pans heat the milk and oil.

First whizz your garlic and a pinch of pepper in the food processor to a fine purée (as once the other ingredients are added you will never get rid of any garlic chippings). Once this is achieved add the cod and potatoes, then have the motor running and add in equal quantities, bit by bit, the hot oil and milk until you achieve the right consistency; a giving, slightly hairy purée.

As a starter serve warm with toast and 8-minute, firmish boiled eggs. As a main course, spread thickly on toast and top with a poached egg.

SKATE, CAPERS AND BREAD

To serve four

a small splash of oil per portion

200g butter

skate wings, seasoned

20 rough 1½cm cubes of yesterday's white bread with the crusts cut off

juice of ½ lemon

a small handful of capers

a small handful of curly parsley, chopped

sea salt and black pepper

If your skate wings are small serve one each, half each if largish, and cut into four if large. The main thing is to make sure your fishmonger skins your wings both sides.

Heat an ovenproof frying pan that's large enough for your fish to lie flat. Apply a spot of oil and a large knob of butter. When sizzling, pop the skate in and *shuggle* the pan slightly to stop the flesh sticking. Turn the fish after a few moments, give the pan another *shuggle*, and place in a hot oven for about 10 minutes. Adjust for the thickness of the skate: your skate is done when the flesh comes easily from the bone when prodded with the point of a knife.

Remove the fish to a warm plate and return the pan to the heat. Add the rest of the butter, wait until this is bubbling, and add the bread cubes. Let these get a little colour, until crispy and buttery, but still giving in the middle. Add the lemon juice, allow it to sizzle and turn brown, and add the capers. At the last minute add the parsley and straight away pour over the fish. Season and serve at once.

All you need now is a spirited salad to follow.

HAIRY TATTIES

To serve six

1.5kg salt ling (see page 214), soaked in frequent changes of cold water for 12 hours

2 onions

3 bay leaves

2kg floury potatoes, e.g. Maris Piper or King Edward, peeled

6 free-range eggs

250ml milk

250g butter

black pepper and possibly sea salt

A splendid dish. If you can't find salt ling, use salt cod, which is a fine substitute.

Put the ling in a pan of fresh water with the onions and bay leaves, bring to the boil, then turn down to a simmer for 14 minutes.

Meanwhile place your potatoes in unsalted water, bring to the boil, and cook until soft enough to mash, and hardboil your eggs so that the yolks are soft and slightly giving.

Drain the fish, discard the onions and bay leaves, and let it cool until you can handle it, then pull the flesh away from the skin and bones – be warned, this is a very sticky exercise.

You should now have warm salt fish and drained hot potatoes. Heat the milk and butter and add half to the potatoes and mash. Add the fish flesh, and keep mashing – you should start to have a pan of hairy mashed potatoes. If they are too stiff add a little more milk and butter. Check for seasoning; it will certainly need black pepper but depending on the fish you may or may not need salt.

Serve a hairy mound with a hardboiled egg, in its shell.

BRILL BAKED ON GREEN AND WHITE VEGETABLES

Feeds three easily

fennel, sliced across the grain

leeks, washed and sliced

onions, peeled and sliced

garlic, peeled and finely chopped

butter

sea salt and black pepper

1 large whole brill, gutted

1–2 lemons

The size of your brill will dictate the number of mouths it will feed. A medium to large brill will satisfy four to six diners, a smallish one two. It should be reasonably large so that it will withstand a cooking time long enough for the vegetables to get to know the fish juices.

You want a whole fish for this, so see what your fishmonger has; also take into account your cooking receptacles and the size of your oven.

In a pan gently sweat your vegetables and garlic in butter, just to start the softening process, but not so that they have given up all resistance. Season. Lay them as a bed for your fish in your dish/oven tray. Place the fish on its vegetable bed, dot with knobs of butter and season, then pop it into a hot oven. Check the fish with a knife – when done the flesh should part easily from the bone. Keep a very close eye after 10 minutes.

Serve with lemon.

GREY MULLET, FENNEL TWIGS AND JERUSALEM ARTICHOKES

To serve two

800g Jerusalem artichokes, washed but not peeled

an 800g grey mullet, gutted and scaled

sea salt and black pepper

a handful of fennel twigs (you can dry these yourself, or some smart fish shops sell them)

a spot of extra virgin olive oil

a big knob of butter

2 lemon halves

There seems an earthy synergy between this fish and the Jerusalem artichoke and, as far as I know, the grey mullet is still plentiful in these days of diminishing fish stocks.

Boil the Jerusalem artichokes in salty water until tender, then drain.

Season the fish liberally inside and out and nustle the fennel twigs into its cavity. Get an ovenproof frying pan (large enough to hold your fish) very hot. Add the oil and butter and allow a little sizzle. Slip your fish in. Wiggle the pan for a moment, so the fish does not stick, then surround it with the boiled Jerusalem artichokes. Roll these around in the butter and pop the pan into a hot oven.

After about 7 minutes, when the fish has turned a convincing colour, turn it over and cook for another 7 minutes. It should be just about there and the artichokes should take on a nutty quality. Serve up with the lemon.

SOFT ROES ON TOAST

To serve four

200g butter

4 pieces of white toast

500g soft roes, still reasonably intact in their sacs

sea salt and black pepper

juice of 1 lemon

chopped curly parsley (optional) – some feel the dish needs this element of green; I do not

Perfect for breakfast, light lunch, high tea or as a savoury with a glass of port. A rich buttery treat.

Soft roes are in fact herring semen, so when filleting a herring for pickling save the soft roes, which are the white creamy sacs, not the granular orange sacs. Otherwise, your fishmonger is bound to have some. Enquire about fresh, although they do freeze very well as long as they are treated properly once defrosted; they need to be handled gently, otherwise they can end up as a creamy mess.

Get a frying pan hot, melt the butter until bubbling, have the toast ready and place the roes in the pan. They will curl up. Cook for 3–4 minutes each side, allowing the roes to brown slightly. Season, and just before placing on the toast, add the lemon juice (and the chopped parsley if you wish) to the now foaming butter.

Place the roes onto the toast, pour the butter over them, and eat.

THREE PIES

CHICKEN AND OX TONGUE PIE
PIKE PIE
EEL PIE JOHNNIE SHAND KYDD
PUFF PASTRY

CHICKEN AND OX TONGUE PIE

To serve four

1 ox tongue, brined for 10–14 days (see page 269)

stock vegetables – an onion, carrot and bundle of herbs

1 happy chicken, poached with onion, leek, black peppercorns and garlic at a gentle simmer for 45 minutes (keep the stock)

2 onions, peeled and sliced

2 large knobs of butter

a handful of plain flour

1.2 litres milk

a big handful of extra-fine capers

sea salt and black pepper

½ quantity of Puff Pastry (see overleaf)

1 egg, lightly beaten

For those of us who sometimes feel a little frail, here is a pie that will sort you out for sure.

Rinse the brined ox tongue and soak it for a couple of hours in fresh water. Poach it very gently for 3 hours with the onion, carrot and bundle of herbs – check it's thoroughly giving. Peel while still warm and cut in half. Use one half for sandwiches and the other for this pie.

Remove the chicken from the bone and cut it into pie-sized chunks. Slice the tongue about 5mm thick, so you will have a chunky chickeny, tonguey weave going on.

Cook the sliced onions in a knob of butter until totally submissive, then mix with the chicken and tongue and place in a pie dish.

Now make your white sauce. Melt the second knob of butter in a pan, add the flour and stir. Do not let it burn or colour but when it smells biscuity, start to add the milk. A whisk is a good thing at this moment. As it thickens, add more milk and whisk again. Hopefully we should end up with about a litre of creamy white sauce, which we let down with a little of the chicken stock and simmer until the word silky comes to mind.

Drain the capers and add to the sauce. Check the sauce for seasoning and pour it over the combination mixture in the pie dish.

Roll out the puff pastry to 7mm thick and use to cover the pie. Brush with the beaten egg and make a small hole in the centre of the pastry. Bake in a hot oven for 30–40 minutes, until well browned.

There we go, frail no longer.

PIKE PIE

The size of your pike might influence your pie size

1 pike

8 leeks, sliced lengthways in half, then cut across at 1cm intervals

2 large knobs of butter

a handful of plain flour

1–2 glasses of white wine

sea salt and black pepper

½ quantity of Puff Pastry (see overleaf)

1 egg, lightly beaten

COURT-BOUILLON

a healthy splash of white wine

a splash of vinegar

2 carrots, chopped

2 celery stalks, chopped

1 onion, peeled and chopped

1 clove of garlic, peeled and chopped

a few black peppercorns

a bay leaf

a few parsley stalks

I always believed there was a huge pike living in Hampstead Ponds that would pull you under and, once you had stopped struggling, would feast upon you. Not a great introduction to pike, mythical or not, but I'm glad to say my pike awareness has come on in leaps and bounds, culminating in Pike Pie.

Find a pan large enough to hold your pike and fill it with water. Add all the court-bouillon ingredients and bring to a simmer. Add the pike and poach gently until it comes easily from the bones. Remove the pike from the court-bouillon, which is now delicious fish stock. Remove the bones and skin from the flesh.

Sweat the chopped leeks in a knob of butter until soft, then mix with the pike flesh and use to fill an appropriate-sized pie dish. You are looking for a good showing of leeks.

Now, follow the previous recipe's advice on white sauce except, once the flour and butter mixture smells biscuity, add the white wine instead of milk. From there on in, add our delicious fish stock until silky springs to mind again. Check for seasoning and pour this sauce over the pike and leeks.

Roll out the puff pastry and use to cover the pie. Brush with the beaten egg and make a small hole in the centre of the pastry. Bake in a hot oven for 30–40 minutes, until well browned.

A magnificent pie.

EEL PIE JOHNNIE
SHAND KYDD

To serve four

1 largish eel (I suggest you get it killed and skinned, neither of which I recommend for the faint-hearted chef)

stock vegetables – 2 onions, 2 carrots, 2 sticks of celery, 2 leeks

1 head of garlic

a bundle of thyme, bay and parsley stalks

½ bottle of white wine

2 healthy knobs of butter, one for the roux and the other for sweating the onions

a handful of plain flour

2 white onions, peeled, cut in half and sliced thinly

a bunch of curly parsley, finely chopped

sea salt and black pepper

Puff Pastry (see opposite)

1 egg, lightly beaten, to paint the top of the pastry

What has happened to the spirit of Peach Melba, Omelette Arnold Bennett and Pigeon Prince Rainier III? The naming of dishes should be reinstated. Here is the eel pie we created for Johnnie's birthday feast.

Cut your eel into 8cm sections. Place these in a pan with the stock vegetables, garlic, herb bundle and the half-bottle of wine and *just* cover with water. Bring this up to a simmer. After half an hour, check your eel – you want its flesh to come away from the bone. When this happens, remove the eel's meat and return the bones to the simmering pot to give up more of the goodness. Another hour should do this, then strain the liquor.

Make a roux with a knob of butter and the flour in a clean pan. Don't let this brown. When it smells biscuity, add ladles of the eel-bone broth, whisking as you go, until you have a kind of liquid, eely silk.

Meanwhile, sweat off your two onions in the second knob of butter until they are sweet and giving but not browned. Add these to the eel meat, which you should have broken into forkable pieces.

Fill your pie dish with the eel and onion mixture, whisk the chopped parsley into your liquid silk, then pour the green liquor over the eel and onions. Season to taste. Roll out the pastry. Pop your puff lid on, paint with the egg, and put into a hot oven for about 25 minutes. Check with a skewer. Serve with mashed potato and raise a glass to Johnnie!

PUFF PASTRY

500g strong white flour

2 tsp sea salt

125g cold unsalted butter, diced,
plus 375g cold unsalted butter

225ml cold water

2 tsp white wine vinegar

Sift the flour into a bowl, then add the salt and the 125g diced butter. Rub the butter in with your fingertips until the mixture looks like breadcrumbs. Add the water and vinegar, and mix to a firm paste. Shape into a ball, wrap in cling film and leave in the fridge overnight.

The next day, take the pastry out of the fridge and leave it to soften for 1–2 hours. The remaining butter should be at the same temperature as the pastry (if the butter is too soft it will melt and ooze out of the pastry, whereas if it is too hard it will break through the pastry and ruin your puff). A good way to achieve the correct temperature is to put the butter between a couple of sheets of baking parchment (or re-use your butter wrappers), beating with a rolling pin to soften it.

When the butter and pastry are ready, roll out your pastry. First roll it into a square, then roll out each side in turn to extend the square into a cross. Leave the centre thick, keeping the ends and sides square. Place the butter in the centre of the pastry, moulding it to the right size if necessary. Then wrap the arms of your cross over and around the butter – start by putting the left arm over the butter, then the right arm over the first arm, next the top and finally the bottom arm. The four arms of your cross should add up to the same thickness as the centre of the pastry. Now you have butter in a pastry package.

Turn your pastry so the top seam is on the right-hand side and roll it out on a floured surface into a rectangle about 20cm wide and 70cm long. Brush the excess flour off, then fold the rectangle in three, like a letter, with one end of the rectangle to the centre and the other end over this. Give the pastry a quarter turn, so the seam is on the right-hand side, then roll out and fold again. Wrap in cling film and leave to rest in the fridge for about 4 hours. Repeat twice more, so you have rolled out the pastry and butter six times, resting it after every two turns. Finally, wrap it in cling film and store in the fridge until ready to use. It also keeps well in the freezer.

VEGETABLES

ORBS OF JOY
WHAT A BAKED POTATO
PRESSED POTATO
GREEN BEANS, SHALLOTS, GARLIC AND ANCHOVIES
SPINACH, DIJON MUSTARD AND CRÈME FRAÎCHE
ROAST TOMATOES AND CROTTINS
MUSHY COURGETTES
ROAST PUMPKIN
BAKED CELERIAC AND EGGS
MASHED PARSNIPS
RADISHES TO ACCOMPANY DUCK OR GOOSE
TURNIP BAKE

ORBS OF JOY

This might sound peculiar but it does make the perfect accompaniment to a grey-legged partridge. One Orb of Joy per person.

Peel some red onions but keep them whole. Put in an oven dish and add chicken stock until they are almost covered. Braise them in a medium oven. As they cook, the stock around them will reduce a little, giving your onions a slightly singed and caramelized exterior and a pale pink and totally giving interior. Truly an orb of joy!

WHAT A BAKED POTATO
To serve four

4 large jacket potatoes

20 cloves of garlic, peeled and left whole

enough duck fat to cover the garlic

sea salt and black pepper

We seem to have moved into the realms of comfort food, and they don't come more comforting than these hot potatoes.

Bake the potatoes in a medium oven until soft to the squeeze. Meanwhile, put the garlic cloves into an ovenproof dish and cover with the duck fat. Cover the dish and put into a gentle to medium oven. Cook until the garlic is totally squishy, then remove from the oven and whizz the garlic and enough of the duck fat in a food processor to give a very loose paste.

Let the potatoes cool enough to handle, then cut them in half lengthways. Scoop out the flesh into a bowl and add the garlic and duck fat paste. Stir thoroughly. When they have combined forces, season and return to the hollow potato skins. Pop into a hot oven until golden brown. Have you ever heard of *such* comforting fare?

PRESSED POTATO

2kg Cyprus potatoes, peeled

a healthy handful of capers (extra-fine if possible)

sea salt and black pepper

How well a potato can deal with discipline.

Boil the potatoes in salted water; check if they are done with a sharp knife in order to catch them before they start to fall apart. Drain.

Line your bread tin or terrine mould with cling film. As soon as the potatoes are at a temperature you can handle, but still warm, slice them 1cm thick. Lay one layer of sliced potato at the bottom of your chosen mould, cautiously sprinkle with capers and salt and pepper, cover this with another layer of potatoes and repeat the caper and seasons. Continue this process until the tin is full, cover with cling film, place a heavy weight on top, the right size to fit within the sides of the mould, and place in the refrigerator overnight.

The next day tip the pressed potato out of its mould and slice with a thin sharp knife.

It is a wonderful base for oily, salty things. For example, you can now dress each slice with anchovy fillets and extra virgin olive oil, hot eel and bacon as on page 210 …

GREEN BEANS, SHALLOTS, GARLIC AND ANCHOVIES

To serve four

2 whole bulbs of garlic

16 shallots, peeled

extra virgin olive oil

sea salt

12 fillets of anchovies in oil, chopped reasonably fine

a handful of capers (extra-fine if possible)

a handful of chopped parsley

a pinch of black pepper

1 tsp red wine vinegar

900g French beans, topped (and if you wish tailed)

Perfect for lamb chops.

Roast the garlic bulbs in a hot oven until they are soft when you squeeze them. Allow to cool to a handleable temperature, then squeeze the flesh out of the cloves. Toss the shallots in a little olive oil on the heat, then place in the oven to roast, keeping a close eye on them and tossing regularly until soft and sweet. Keep warm.

Put a pan of well-salted water on to boil. Mix the anchovies with the garlic flesh, capers, parsley and pepper. Add a splash of extra virgin olive oil and the vinegar.

When the water is boiling, put the beans in and boil for 4 minutes. Check they are to your liking, drain, then mix them in a warm bowl with the shallots and anchovy dressing.

Serve straight away with lamb chops (which hopefully you have not forgotten to cook while doing all the above).

SPINACH, DIJON MUSTARD AND CRÈME FRAÎCHE

a big bag of spinach, stalks removed, washed, then cooked down in butter

a healthy spoonful of Dijon mustard

a handful of grated hard sheep's milk cheese or Parmesan

a dollop of crème fraîche

sea salt and black pepper

This is a splendid dollop of green with a difference. All you need is a food processor to whizz the ingredients.

It is as easy as whizzing all the ingredients together, then eating. Do not refrigerate.

It has numerous companions, meat, fish or fowl, and everyone goes yum!

ROAST TOMATOES AND CROTTINS

For six

18–24 vine tomatoes (if possible, or if not the most delicious tomatoes available to you), depending on how large your tomatoes are

sea salt and black pepper

20 cloves of garlic, peeled

extra virgin olive oil

6 crottins

a large bunch of fresh mint, leaves only

juice of 1 lemon

a pile of white, long crispy toast made by slicing the bread, drizzling with extra virgin olive oil, and baking on a tray in the oven until golden brown at the edges and crispy

A crottin is a small, button-like goat's cheese from France, some for eating and others specifically for cooking with. For a while now a few British goat's cheese makers have been producing them. St. John uses crottins from a goatherd in Barnet, surprisingly, so look out, there could be a crottin producer near you!

Place the tomatoes in an oven dish, season with salt and pepper, scatter your garlic, and then, in a generous fashion, splash your olive oil over all. Put into a hot oven for approximately 25 minutes until the tomatoes are soft and giving. Remove from the oven and check that the garlic is soft and cooked; if not, remove the tomatoes onto a plate and pop the garlic back into the oven until cooked. Once ready return the tomatoes to the dish. Nestle in your crottins and return to the oven until they are giving but not gone. Once again, remove from the oven.

Slightly tear your mint leaves and dress with the lemon juice and a splash of extra virgin olive oil. Season with salt and pepper, place in a clump on top of your tomatoes and crottins, and serve with the pile of crispy toast.

Squish the tomato, garlic, crottin, and mint onto the toast, scoop up some of the garlicky, tomatoey oil, and eat.

MUSHY COURGETTES
To serve six

115g butter

4 cloves of garlic, peeled and very finely chopped

900g courgettes, topped and tailed, then sliced into rounds 8mm thick

sea salt and black pepper

In the day and age of the *al dente* vegetable, what a joy to find a recipe that celebrates the well-cooked, buttery vegetable.

On a gentle heat, melt the butter and sweat the garlic (making sure it does not brown or burn). Add the courgettes, season carefully, and toss in the garlicky butter. Cover and continue the gentle cooking, stirring occasionally. After 15 minutes uncover. When some of the courgette slices start to break, binding the whole together, check the seasoning, and serve.

ROAST PUMPKIN

Keep an eye on it.

What is vital here is the pumpkin. It must be an organic blue pumpkin, which can be obtained at health-food shops. Once you have tried one, the large, orange, woolly variety will become a thing of the past in your life.

As to the roasting, simply cut it in half, scoop out the seeds, then cut into moon crescents. Place the pieces on a baking tray, skin down, drizzle with extra virgin olive oil, season with salt and pepper, and roast in a hot oven, basting occasionally. This should take about 20–25 minutes. Check with a knife to see when it's soft.

Be careful not to overcook your pumpkin as it will dry out.

BAKED CELERIAC
AND EGGS

To serve four

1 large head of celeriac or 2 small, peeled and cut into chunks

225g butter, approximately

sea salt and black pepper

the leaves of a head of celery, chopped

8 free-range eggs

A wintery lunch that is not dark brown and meaty.

Place the celeriac in a pan of well-salted water, bring to the boil, and cook for approximately 25 minutes; check with a knife. When cooked, drain the celeriac – make a thorough job of this as you do not want a watery celeriac mash.

On a gentle heat mash the celeriac in a pan with butter, adding as much as you feel the celeriac wants to absorb. Season to taste.

Now mix the celery leaves into the celeriac. Decant this mixture into a warm oven dish, and make eight indents in the surface of the mash, into which break eight eggs. Season the eggs and place two small knobs of butter on top. Bake in a hot oven for approximately 5 minutes, keeping an eye on it, until the egg whites are firmed up, but the yolks are still runny. Serve right away.

MASHED PARSNIPS

To serve six

1.35kg parsnips, peeled
and cut in half

1.1 litres milk

sea salt

285g butter

black pepper

Rich, sweet and soothing.

Boil the parsnips in the milk with a pinch of salt. When cooked, drain them, reserving the milk. Mash with the butter. If they seem too dry add a splash of cooking milk. Season to taste and serve.

RADISHES TO ACCOMPANY DUCK OR GOOSE

To serve six

3 bunches of radishes with
happy leaves

juices from the roasting pan of the
duck or goose or duck fat and
a splash of chicken stock

sea salt and black pepper

The fresh, peppery radishes make a perfect foil for the rich birds.

Remove the leaves from the radishes and wash both the leaves and the radishes. Heat up your roasting juices or fat and stock, then add the radishes. Let this sizzle, stirring frequently. In approximately 5 minutes the radishes will have changed to pink blushing orbs, still crispy but with a hint of giving. Add the radish leaves and remove the pan from the heat. These do two things: they give a wonderful flavour, and they add a structural weave, preventing your radishes from rolling all over your plate when served. Season and stir, letting the leaves wilt a moment, then serve with roast duck or goose.

TURNIP BAKE

To serve six

1 onion, peeled and sliced very thinly

200g butter

1.2kg turnips, peeled and sliced very thinly

sea salt and black pepper

This may sound like a grim dish in a grim vegetarian café, but it is not. Unfortunately I have not been able to think up a more tempting name for this delicious dish yet.

In a pan sweat the onion in 150g of the butter until it's soft, sweet and clear. Put to one side. Smear the remaining butter over a deep ovenproof frying pan, into which you place the first layer of sliced turnip. Add a smattering of your buttery onion mixture, season, follow with another layer of turnip, and repeat this process until the frying pan is full (the turnips will shrink during cooking, do not be disappointed).

Cover with tinfoil (shiny side down; the matt side encourages the transference of heat through the foil whereas the shiny side will deflect it slightly, which at other times is just what you want). Place into a medium to hot oven for approximately 1 hour so it is thoroughly cooked. Check for a giving centre with a knife. When satisfied take out of the oven, remove the foil and allow it to calm down for about 5 minutes.

Now to serve, tip it upside down onto the appropriate-sized plate (being careful not to burn yourself in this manoeuvre). You should now have a brown and yielding turnip bake (it will not be crisp), calling out to be eaten with some roast lamb.

DRESSINGS, SAUCES AND PICKLES

TOMATO KETCHUP
HORSERADISH SAUCE
TARTARE SAUCE
MINT SAUCE
MAYONNAISE
AÏOLI
VINAIGRETTE
GREEN SAUCE AND ITS POSSIBILITIES
MUSTARD DRESSING FOR GREENS
ANCHOVY DRESSING
ST. JOHN CHUTNEY
GREEN BEAN CHUTNEY
PICKLED SHALLOTS
PICKLED GHERKINS

TOMATO KETCHUP

Makes enough for many fish and chips

3.5kg tomatoes, roughly chopped

1kg apples, peeled, cored and chopped

6 onions, peeled and chopped

800g sugar

1 litre malt vinegar

2 tbsp sea salt

1 tsp cayenne pepper

12 black peppercorns

12 whole allspice

12 cloves

You will need a stainless-steel pan, large enough for all the ingredients. Tie the peppercorns, allspice and cloves in a muslin or stockinet. This ketchup will improve with age.

Place all the ingredients in the pan, bring to a boil, and reduce to a simmer; you want to cook until the ingredients are a pulp, which should take approximately 2 hours. Remove from the heat and press through a sieve. Return the resulting mixture to the pan and heat to reunite it after its pressing experience. Boil for 2 or 3 minutes and then decant into sterilized jars (see page 317) and seal. Allow it a few days to find its feet, and then it is ready to use in all its many ways.

HORSERADISH SAUCE

Makes about 350ml

13cm piece of fresh horseradish, peeled

juice of ½ lemon

300ml crème fraîche

sea salt and black pepper

A very fine thing.

Finely grate the horseradish. This can be quite an emotional experience and may bring tears to your eyes, but is very good for clearing the tubes. Sprinkle the grated horseradish with lemon juice to prevent it discolouring. Mix gently with the crème fraîche and season to taste.

It's ready.

TARTARE SAUCE

Makes one bowlful

300ml Mayonnaise of a firmish nature (see overleaf)

a handful of capers (extra-fine if possible) – make sure these are well drained

a handful of cornichons, chopped in a coarse fashion, not into round or long sections

2 hardboiled free-range eggs, peeled and chopped neither too fine nor too coarse

3 sprigs of tarragon, picked and chopped

a small handful of curly parsley, chopped

I realize this is old hat, but there are so many strange versions of this classic sauce served that I feel it is justified for me to add my recipe to the fray.

Mix all the ingredients together and serve.

MINT SAUCE

Plenty for a roast leg of lamb

1 tsp Demerara sugar

2 tsp malt vinegar (keep it close at hand in case a splash more is needed)

1 tsp boiling water

a bunch of mint, picked and finely chopped

Another classic sauce which has been chronicled many a time, but I recently made it and found it so good, I cannot resist mentioning it.

Dissolve the Demerara sugar in the vinegar, with the aid of the boiling water. Pour over the mint and mix. If you feel it is too dry, or not sharp enough, adjust with a little more malt vinegar.

MAYONNAISE

Makes about 600ml

3 free-range egg yolks

2 tsp Dijon mustard

sea salt

about 600ml extra virgin olive oil

a healthy splash of lemon juice

a healthy splash of white wine vinegar

freshly ground black pepper

You can use a food processor, or a mortar and pestle, or a bowl and wooden spoon. Some use vegetable oil rather than olive oil for a gentler result. I do not. Your mayonnaise should have that bitter olive taste. Some thin with water; I feel this should be avoided.

Place the egg yolks, mustard and a gesture of salt in the food processor, mortar or bowl. Mix, then drizzle oil in very slowly, especially at the beginning so as you achieve an emulsified mixture. You can add up to 600ml oil; if you feel confident that the emulsification will hold, continue adding oil. If it is getting too thick add a splash of lemon juice and white wine vinegar, you can always add more oil. Season to taste.

After a while you will learn the various noises mayonnaise makes in the making which tell you when you have enough oil; these are hard to describe in words so I'm afraid you just have to listen to it. You want a consistency that has a body to it, but a body with give, not one which goes *boing* when you put a spoon in it.

If you are using a mortar and pestle, or bowl and spoon, follow the same process, but I stress the importance of the most gentle of drizzling of oil with this method.

AÏOLI

Makes about 600ml

20 *cloves of garlic*

sea salt and black pepper

2 *free-range egg yolks*

at least 600ml extra virgin olive oil

juice of 2 lemons (you may not need all the juice but it is best to have it to hand)

Aïoli often seems to be mistaken for a garlic mayonnaise, but this is not so. Aïoli is aïoli and eating it should be an emotional experience – it is strong, but that is its role in life. Purists would disagree, but I find a food processor very useful here; the final consistency seems to hold together better. The instructions assume you will too, but if you prefer there is always the mortar and pestle. Purists may also disagree about the inclusion of eggs. Sorry.

Put the garlic into the chopping bowl with a pinch of salt (this helps to break it up) and pepper, then whizz until finely pulped – this is important as you do not want garlic chippings in the aïoli. Add the egg yolks, let them meet the garlic for a moment, then carefully and slowly add the oil in a gentle stream. The emulsion should safely hold up to 300ml oil; at this point take a view and, if you can, add a little more oil. Now add the lemon juice, tasting as you go, adjust the seasoning, then refrigerate.

VINAIGRETTE

Makes approximately 300ml

2 cloves of garlic

1 tbsp Dijon mustard

a pinch of sea salt and black pepper

juice of 1 lemon

2 tsp white wine vinegar

300ml extra virgin olive oil

You can do this in a food processor or by hand.

Crush your garlic (making sure this is finely done, as you don't want chips of garlic in your dressing), add the mustard, salt and pepper, lemon juice, and vinegar, then, as you mix, slowly add the olive oil so you get an emulsion. Once all the oil is added check the dressing for taste; you can add more salt and pepper, lemon juice or vinegar to taste at this point.

The lemon juice and vinegar used together seem to set each other off, avoiding a too bitter lemon result, and the juice tempers the vinegar rather in the same magical way whiskey and lemon juice meet in a whiskey sour, both becoming something else altogether. This keeps very well in the fridge.

GREEN SAUCE AND ITS POSSIBILITIES

Plenty for six

half a bunch of curly parsley

half a bunch of flat-leaf parsley

half a bunch of mint

a quarter-bunch of dill

a small showing of tarragon (it has a habit of taking over if added in too large quantities)

1 small tin of anchovy fillets, finely chopped

12 cloves of garlic, peeled and finely chopped

a handful of capers, roughly chopped (if extra-fine keep whole)

extra virgin olive oil

crushed black pepper

Green Sauce is a wonderful thing and goes with almost every meat, roast, boiled or cold, vegetables, and some fish. Its companions know no bounds. The parsleys are essential, the other herbs good additions; rejig the parsley if you're not including any of them. Never use a food processor to make Green Sauce, you will end up with a pulp rather than a textural delight.

Chop your herbs finely, but not too finely, and mix with the anchovy, garlic and capers. Add olive oil to reach a loose, still spoonable, but not runny or oily consistency. Taste and season with black pepper (the anchovies should negate any necessity for salt).

ITS POSSIBILITIES

There are many things you can add to this sauce: chopped cornichons (but do this just before serving as it tends to discolour the sauce if left standing) and chopped egg are two of the finest.

Depending how coarsely you chop your herbs, if at all even, it can become more of a salad than a sauce. Or, on the other hand, it makes a splendid salad dressing when diluted by the addition of more oil or vinaigrette.

You have five wonderful things:

Capers
Anchovies
Extra virgin olive oil
Garlic
Parsley

There is no end to the possibilities …

MUSTARD DRESSING FOR GREENS

Makes just over 250ml

3 tsp Dijon mustard

1 tsp red wine vinegar

150ml extra virgin olive oil

sea salt and black pepper

This simple dressing just gives a lift to greens and is perfect with pork sausages, Bath Chaps (see page 94) or bacon chops. It keeps well in the fridge.

Mix the ingredients together and toss your boiled greens in the mixture. Serve immediately so that the greens do not cool down.

ANCHOVY DRESSING

Makes approximately 300ml

7 garlic cloves, peeled
a pinch of black pepper
1 tin of anchovies in oil
285ml extra virgin olive oil
a splash of red wine vinegar

A food processor or a mortar and pestle is important for this recipe.

Place the garlic and pepper into a food processor or mortar and crush to a fine purée, then add the anchovies and allow them to break down. Start to add the oil, then the vinegar to taste. Check the flavour for seasoning.

This dressing, depending on how thick you make it, can have many uses.

With less oil and vinegar added you will have a very firm mix which is delicious spread on toast and eaten with sweet roasted shallots. If the full amount of oil and vinegar is added you should have a looser, though still emulsified mixture, which is ideal for dressing boiled greens or broccoli (which can be eaten on their own or with lamb or beef), or it makes excellent dressing for raw bitter salad leaves.

ST. JOHN CHUTNEY

Makes enough to fill a dozen jam jars

Spice Bag (see page 269)

1.5kg apples, peeled, cored and chopped

1kg bag of shallots, peeled

10 cloves of garlic, peeled

1.5kg tomatoes, chopped

1kg dates

1kg raisins

200g pieces of fresh ginger, peeled and coarsely grated

1kg soft dark brown sugar, or to taste

600ml malt vinegar, or to taste

There is nothing finer, after having a good stock up your sleeve, than having a reserve of chutney.

Take a large stainless-steel pot, with a thick bottom so as not to be affected by the vinegar, and bring all the ingredients together. Cook on a gentle heat, stirring occasionally to avoid sticking at the bottom, for about 1 hour. What you want is a brown chutney look and consistency – this may take some more cooking, but be careful not to go too far: you do not want to end up with a brown, jammy consistency. When satisfied, remove the spice bag and bottle in clean, sealable sterilized jars (see page 317) and refrigerate for at least two weeks before eating.

GREEN BEAN CHUTNEY

Makes between five and six jam jars

900g runner beans, trimmed and cut into 1½cm diagonal lengths

675g shallots, chopped

575ml malt vinegar

675g Demerara sugar

1½ tsp sea salt

1 tsp dry English mustard

1½ tbsp dried turmeric

2 tbsp cornflour

This recipe comes from Joan Chapman, who has won many a prize with her chutneys and vegetables at the Great Bedwyn Village Fête, so we are in very capable hands.

Cook the beans for 5 minutes in salted water and drain. Cook the shallots in half the vinegar for 10 minutes, then add everything except the cornflour and the remaining vinegar, and cook slowly for approximately 30 minutes. Mix the cornflour with the remaining vinegar, add, and cook for a further 10 minutes, stirring constantly. Decant into clean, sterilized sealable jars (see page 317) and keep for a few weeks, if you can, before eating.

PICKLED SHALLOTS

For 1kg shallots

sea salt

malt vinegar

white wine vinegar

8 cloves

10 allspice

2 cinnamon sticks, whole

8 white peppercorns

10 black peppercorns

4 bay leaves

12 coriander seeds

4 small hot dried chilli peppers

A version of the pickled onion which makes lively company for meats hot or cold, and cheese. Use small round shallots, peeled but left whole.

Cover the shallots with brine (made with 500g salt to 1.5 litres water) and leave to soak in a plastic, glass or china container for a week in the fridge.

Now you know how much liquid it takes to cover your shallots, heat the same amount of a mixture of half and half malt vinegar and white wine vinegar in a stainless-steel pan with the collection of spices. While this comes up to the simmer, rinse the shallots thoroughly and then place into the simmering spiced vinegar for 5 minutes then remove from the heat and bottle in clean, sterilized sealable jars (see page 317) and keep for a month somewhere cool. They are now ready to use. The leftover spiced vinegar is very good for dipping cooked whelks in.

PICKLED GHERKINS

For 2kg gherkins

200g sea salt

pickling spice (you can buy this already mixed), which should include celery seed, mustard seed, black peppercorns, small dried red chilli, coriander seed and dill seed

800g sugar

3 tbsp acetic acid

1.1 litres water

An incredibly useful thing to have up your sleeve. After many failures in the restaurant at pickling gherkins, Anna Rottman, a friend of my wife's in New Zealand, showed me the way.

Wash your gherkins, sprinkle them with salt, and leave to stand for 2–3 hours, occasionally tossing them gently. Shake off the salt and place the gherkins in a bowl, cover with clean boiling water, and leave them to stand for 5 minutes. Drain.

Place the gherkins in clean, sterilized sealable jars, adding a healthy, many-fingered pinch of pickling spice to each jar. Meanwhile place the sugar, acid and water into a stainless-steel pan and boil until the sugar and acid have dissolved. Pour hot over the gherkins.

Seal the jars while the liquor is still hot. Keep in your cupboard for at least a month before eating.

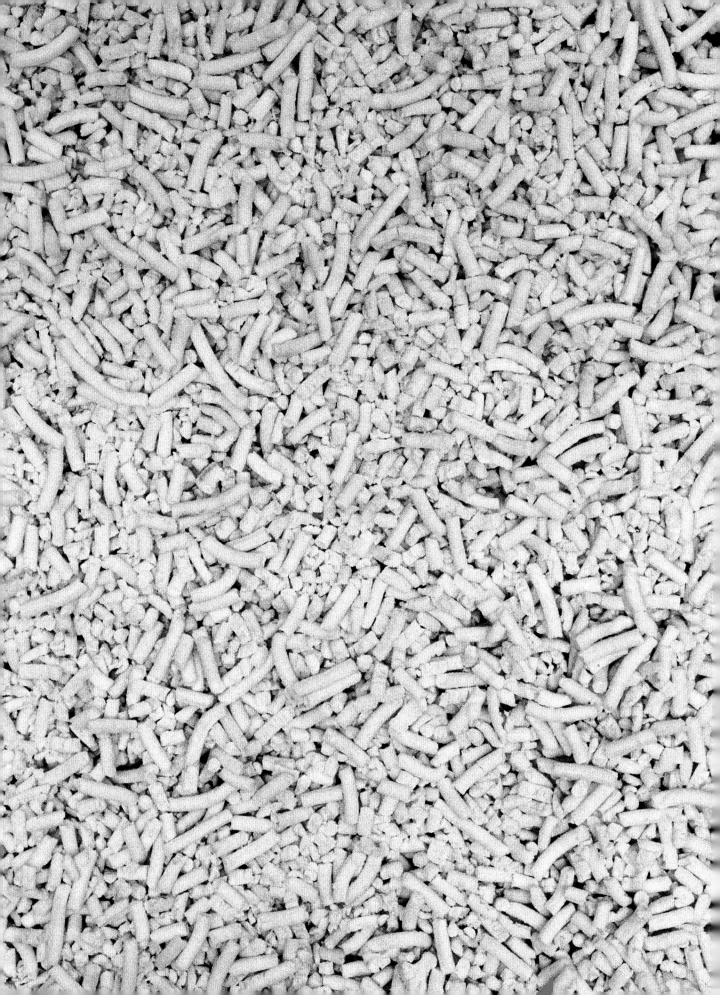

BASIC, BUT VITAL

BASIC STOCKS
TO CLARIFY BROTH
MAKING A BRINE
SPICE BAG
RENDERING

BASIC STOCKS

Stock is fundamental, but it's also easy. All you have to do is remember to keep your bones, giblets and shells. There is almost nothing as reassuring as having some stock up your sleeve.

Stock vegetables can be defined by what you have to hand, though you should not be too cavalier in your approach to stock, and it does not take too much trouble to have the right vegetables: onions (with skin on, chopped in half); a bulb of garlic (with skin on, chopped in half); carrots (peeled and split lengthways); a leek (split lengthways and cleaned); fennel; celery and its leaf; red onions (skin on and cut in half if you want a darker stock); mushroom peelings if you have some to hand; a bay leaf; herbs, or simply the stalks, say, if you have picked some parsley; peppercorns. Please feel free to express yourself.

The other essential ingredient is water; you want to cover your stock ingredients with enough to allow for skimming (which is vital), but not so much as to drown any possible flavour. Bring to a simmer, but not a rolling boil as this will boil the surface scum back into the stock. I shall again say SKIM. To know when a stock is ready, taste and taste again, though the timings given below should be a good guide. Have the bones and vegetables released their goodness? Each creature's stock benefits from its own particular approach.

Once you have your finished stock you have the further option of clarifying it, which is the process of completely clearing it of fat and particles. Some would say the perfect broth should have glistening spots of fat on the surface, to be supped up with your bread. Certainly clarification is not essential, and then again, sometimes there is a certain splendour in a completely clear broth.

Remember: if you have boiled a chicken, ham or beef, do not throw away the broth. You have created a stock for the next day.

The bits we add to vegetables and water:

CHICKEN

You can simply use the carcass of your roast chicken, or your butcher will be able to supply you with chicken bones. Chicken wings are particularly good for stock, as are the giblets and neck if your chicken comes with them. This should take approximately 1½–2 hours.

DUCK AND GOOSE

These should come with their giblets and neck. Use these, and once you have eaten your bird you can use the carcass. Similarly with game birds: hang on to their little frames once you have eaten the flesh, and pop them in the stock pot. These, too, should take about 1½–2 hours.

VEAL

All good butchers will have veal bones. Ask them to cut them up slightly, allowing the goodness from the heart of the bones to emerge and enrich your stock. Roast the bones to a golden brown in the oven before putting them in the pot with the vegetables (red onions would be appropriate here) and water. Due to the size of the bones this stock will need to simmer longer than the others, about 3 hours. At this point you have veal stock that you can use as it is or reduced. I myself am not a fan of the brown sticky reductions (jus) that many chefs seem partial to, so the following is as brown and sticky as I get – you can get a lot stickier. Brown a new selection of vegetables (including red onion) in a little oil in a pan, then pour in red wine (how much depends on how much stock you have, so at this point you have to make an educated guess as to how much wine your pot needs – between a quarter and a third of the volume of stock) and allow this to reduce by two-thirds. Now add the veal stock. Bring this to a simmer and allow it to reduce by half (stop if it seems to be getting too viscous). You now have a rich brown veal reduction.

FISH

For fish stock, if you are not filleting fish at home ask your fishmonger for the bones and heads of non-oily fish and remove their gills. I am sure if you ask nicely your fishmonger will do this for you. This may prove difficult, as the wet fish shop seems to be disappearing, in which case, buy yourself some cheap white not fatty fish. If you are lucky enough to come by it, conger eel is very good. As regards the vegetables, in the case of fish stock I stick to the green and white varieties. In a little oil sweat your heads, bones or fish bits, allowing them to colour but not burn. Add the vegetables and water. Bring to a simmer, being careful not to boil them, which will give a harsh fish flavour. Approximately 45–60 minutes should do. If you're planning to eat crabs, lobsters, langoustines, even prawns, keep all their shells, as they make a splendid stock. Place the shells in a pot and crush with a hammer, or the end of a heavy wooden rolling pin, until you have a shelly pulp. In this case, chop your vegetables a mite finer than I have previously recommended, and sweat them in a little oil, not browning, until they are soft and sweet. Add a couple of tinned plum tomatoes (not enough to make it tomatoey), crushing them in your hands.

Add the shell pulp and sweat until you smell splendid shellfish things. Add water and simmer until the shells have released their flavour, approximately 1½–2 hours. When it comes time to strain, ladle the broth and pulp into a sieve and bash it through with the bowl of the ladle, then discard the dry beaten remains in the sieve.

CHICKPEA

The water you have cooked chickpeas in makes an excellent vegetarian stock.

TO CLARIFY BROTH

For 2 litres broth

450g raw lean flesh, from the same creature as your broth (this helps the flavour of your broth; the clarification might very slightly dent its flavour)

1 large or 2 small leeks, cleaned

2 egg whites and their shells

2 litres cold stock

Here is a basic clarification recipe.

In a food processor, whizz the meat, leeks and egg whites and shells into a pulp. Whisk this mixture into your cold (preferably fridge cold) broth in a pan, place on the heat and bring to a gentle simmer. Do not stir again. What will be happening is similar to making coffee in a cafetière, but in reverse. The meat and egg form a sieve layer, which will rise through the broth, collecting any detritus on its way, until it forms a crust on top of the broth. This is why the most gentle of simmering is required, otherwise the crust will break up and be boiled back into the broth.

Once the crust has become reasonably firm, keep the pan on a gentle heat, otherwise the crust will sink, and lift it off with a slotted spoon. Finally, if your broth is not clear, then complete the process by straining it through muslin or a very fine sieve.

MAKING A BRINE

Makes 4 litres

400g caster sugar (many suggest brown sugar, but not me)

600g sea salt

12 juniper berries

12 cloves

12 black peppercorns

3 bay leaves

4 litres water

You can use your brine to preserve many of the meats you will use in this book, e.g. pork belly, beef brisket or silverside, or ox tongue. Some recommend saltpetre instead of sea salt; I always feel it is a little too ferocious, and as a result am aware of it at the eating stage.

Bring all the brine ingredients together in a pot, and bring to the boil so the sugar and salt melt. Decant into a container and allow to cool. When cold add your meat, and leave it in the brine for the number of days required for your recipe.

SPICE BAG

whole black peppercorns

whole coriander seeds

whole white peppercorns

whole chillies

allspice

mace

bay leaf

celery seeds

cloves

fennel seeds

mustard seeds

Spice containment.

To avoid crunching on an emotional peppercorn or cautiously extracting a collation of sturdy seeds from your mouth, tie ingredients together in a stockinet bag.

RENDERING

Traditionally, being a seafaring nation, preserving food in Britain
has always been important; unfortunately, the deep freeze has eclipsed
the process of rendering, cooking and preserving in fat, which produces
tender, flavoursome meat that keeps, improving with age, and could
not be more versatile in its gastronomic possibilities.

In the sixteenth century, for long sea journeys, cooked ducks and
mallards were preserved in their own fat, butter and spices. In France
the practice of confit (cooking and preserving meat in fat) has
remained fundamental in modern kitchens. In Britain potting meat
(cooking meat, shredding it, and covering it with an airtight layer
of butter or suet) is still popular. But, for a country full of ducks and
geese, why are we not using the fat like the sixteenth-century navy?

Duck and geese are extraordinary fat providers. Put your hand into
their cavity and you should be able to pull out a great clump of fat;
place this into a pan and heat to a melting simmer. When it appears
all the fat has flown, strain it into a jar, seal it and allow it to cool,
then refrigerate. Using the same method you can also render down
pork fat. Roast a duck and see how fat collects into your roasting tray.
Again, pour this off into a jar, seal it, allow it to cool then refrigerate.
If you still need more fat you can always buy tins of duck or goose fat.

HOW TO DO IT
In a plastic, glass or china container, scantily scatter sea salt, black
pepper and twigs of thyme. Place a layer of your chosen meat and
repeat your scattering. Keep on layering until done. Cover and leave
in the fridge for 24 hours. This, as well as flavouring it, removes water
from the meat. The next day there should be a salty puddle in your
container. Remove the meat and brush off any remaining salt,
pepper and thyme. Dry it with a clean tea towel, place in an oven
dish or pan, cover with duck, goose or pork fat, or a combination,
and cover with foil.

Cook in a medium oven until the flesh is giving but not falling apart. When it's cooked, remove the meat to a sealable glass, plastic or china container, then pour fat over to cover. Seal the container, allow it to cool and refrigerate. The only exception is tongue, which, while warm, should be peeled then returned to the fat.

WHAT TO DO WITH YOUR GOODIES IN FAT

Your meat is now flavoursome, giving and amazingly versatile. Duck, goose or rabbit legs are a meal in themselves when heated in a hot oven to crisp the skin, or sorted through and shredded in a salad. So, too, with giblets; use warmed in a salad, in a terrine, in stews – the possibilities hold no bounds. If cooking a lentil or bean stew the confit of pork belly or skin could not be anywhere happier. Eat tongues (at room temperature so the fat can run off) sliced with pickles or in a salad, pan-fry slices or make a kind of rich pressed tongue by placing the warm tongue into a terrine mould or cling-film-lined bread tin, drizzling over some of the fat, and putting under great pressure.

You can then reuse the fat for preserving or cooking with. Restaurants are confiting madly, and so should you at home.

APPROXIMATE COOKING TIMES IN FAT

Ducks' legs: 2¼ hours

Goose legs: 2¾ hours

Duck or goose gizzards, necks, hearts: 2 hours

Rabbits' legs: 2 hours

Lambs' tongues: 2 hours

Pigs' tongues: 2½ hours

Pork belly: 2½ hours

Pork skin: 1½ hours

KEEPING TIMES

Food preserved in fat has fantastic longevity, if kept in the fridge and properly covered in fat, but nature being nature there is now and then a batch that does not wish to grow old gracefully. So this method of preserving is not for ever, and I recommend using within six months.

I now pass you over to the very capable hands of Justin,
to explore the world of Pastry, Pudding and Bread.

BREAD

MOTHER
OLD DOUGH
WHITE LOAF
WHOLEMEAL LOAF
WHITE SOURDOUGH LOAF
BROWN SOURDOUGH LOAF
RAISIN LOAF
SANDWICH LOAF
SODA BREAD

MOTHER

1 stick of rhubarb

210ml water

2 tbsp live yoghurt

50g rye flour

50g wholemeal flour

100g strong white flour

The Mother forms the base of all our breads at St. John (except soda bread). We started ours about five years ago and have been looking after her ever since.

A Mother adds character to your bread. The flavour and texture of sourdough in particular come from using no commercial yeast, only your Mother. The process takes longer but the results are worth the wait.

DAY 1

Chop the rhubarb into slices 5mm thick and mix with the water and yoghurt. Add the flour and stir until you have a wet, lumpy mixture. Place in a clean container, dust with white flour and leave somewhere warm (around 26–28°C).

DAY 2

Just give the mixture a stir and dust with white flour again.

DAY 3

Stir it again; you should see signs of fermentation taking place. Add 4 tablespoons of white flour and 4 tablespoons of water, mix well and dust with white flour.

DAYS 4–5

On Day 4, discard about a third of the Mother and replace with a fresh quantity of all the ingredients except the rhubarb. Repeat on Day 5.

DAY 6

The Mother should now be ready to use in your bread making – it should be bubbly and smell strong and sour.

After making a loaf, you will need to replenish the Mother with half and half flour and water, in equal quantities to the amount you took out – so if you make the White Loaf (see overleaf) for example, which uses 100g of the Mother, you would have to replace it with 50g flour and 50ml water. The type of flour you use for replenishment depends on which loaf you plan to make next: for a white loaf use strong white flour; for brown, use 25g strong white flour and 25g wholemeal flour.

After replenishing, leave the Mother to ferment for a day before use. You can leave it in the fridge without feeding for months but it will take a few days to restart it by feeding it – again, discard about a third and feed it equal parts flour and water. Repeat this until there are signs of fermentation.

OLD DOUGH

1.25kg strong white flour

750ml water

5g fresh yeast

Like the Mother, above, Old Dough adds flavour and texture to a loaf.

Mix all the ingredients together, either by hand or in a machine, until well incorporated. Place in an oiled plastic container and leave in the fridge for 24 hours before use.

WHITE LOAF

520g strong white flour

100g Mother (see page 276)

340ml water (at 5°C)

½ tsp fresh yeast

60ml cold water (the bathe)

10g sea salt

Bread is as vital as your knife and fork in the eating process.

MAKING THE DOUGH

Place the flour, Mother, water and yeast in an electric mixer and, using the dough hook attachment, mix on low speed for 6 minutes, until all the water is incorporated and the dough starts to leave the sides of the bowl clean. Leave to stand for 5 minutes, then start pouring in the bathe. We do this in three goes: begin by adding a third of the bathe and mix the dough for 4 minutes on low speed. Repeat with the next third of the bathe. Add the final third of the bathe and mix for 6 minutes, until the dough looks smooth. Leave it to rest for 10 minutes. Then add the salt and mix for 4 minutes, again until the dough looks smooth and leaves the sides of the bowl clean.

RISING

The dough will be quite wet. Roll it into a ball, return it to the mixing bowl and sprinkle with flour. Cover with a cloth, place in the fridge and leave for 1 hour.

Remove the dough from the fridge, shape it into a ball again, sprinkle with flour and cover. Leave it somewhere warm (about 20°C, or warm room temperature) for 3 hours, until slightly risen.

Take your dough and either shape it into one large ball or split it in half for two smaller loaves. Place on a floured baking tray, sprinkle with flour and cover. Leave to rest for 15 minutes.

SHAPING

We shape the loaf into a baton but you can choose your own shape and style. Try not to use too much flour when rolling, as it gets into the dough, leaving pockets of raw flour in the loaf. Once you have shaped it, place it on a baking sheet, sprinkle with flour and cover. Leave for 1–2 hours, until doubled in size.

BAKING

Preheat the oven to 230°C/Gas Mark 8. Place a heatproof bowl of water on the bottom of the oven. This will produce steam, which will form a better crust.

Remove the cloth from the bread and, using a very sharp knife or better, a razor blade, slash the top three times lengthways at an angle. Then place the loaf in the oven and bake for 30 minutes. Open the oven door to let out excess steam, take out your bowl of water, then close the door and bake for 10 minutes more. To test if the loaf is done, turn over and tap on the base; if it sounds hollow it is ready. Place on a wire rack to cool.

WHOLEMEAL LOAF

300g wholemeal flour
200g strong white flour
100g Mother (see page 276)
340ml water (at 5°C)
½ tsp fresh yeast
75ml cold water (the bathe)
10g sea salt

Make as for the White Loaf (see opposite) but take note: the dough will be firmer. We like to finish a wholemeal loaf by slashing a single cut along its length before baking.

WHITE SOURDOUGH LOAF

500g strong white flour

130g Mother (see page 276)

320ml water (at 5°C)

90ml cold water (the bathe)

10g sea salt

The offspring of Justin's much-nurtured Mother.

MAKING THE DOUGH

Place the flour, Mother and water in an electric mixer and, using the dough hook attachment, mix on low speed for 6 minutes, making sure all the water is incorporated and the dough starts to leave the sides of the bowl clean. Then begin to pour in the bathe. Do this a third at a time, as we do for the White Loaf (see page 280). Leave the dough to rest for 20 minutes. Then add the salt and mix for 4 minutes, again until the dough looks smooth and leaves the sides of the bowl clean.

RISING

Shape the dough into a ball, then place it back in the mixing bowl and sprinkle with flour. Cover with a cloth, place in the fridge and leave for 1 hour.

Remove the dough from the fridge, shape it into a ball again, sprinkle with flour and cover. Then leave it somewhere warm (about 20°C, or warm room temperature) for about 3 hours, until slightly risen.

Take the dough and either shape it into one large ball or split it in half for two smaller loaves. Place on a floured tray, sprinkle with flour and cover. Leave to rest for 15 minutes.

SHAPING

We shape sourdough loaves into a ball but you can choose your own shape and style. Place the shaped loaf in a floured proving basket or a floured plastic bowl and sprinkle with flour. Cover with a cloth and leave for 4–5 hours, until doubled in size.

BAKING

Preheat the oven to 230°C/Gas Mark 8. Place a heatproof bowl of water on the bottom of the oven. This will produce steam, which will form a better crust.

Take the cloth off the bread and carefully transfer the loaf to a baking sheet. Using a razor blade or a very sharp knife (a razor blade is best), slash a cut round the circumference of the loaf in a single movement. Then place it in the oven and bake for 30 minutes. Open the oven door to let out any excess steam and take out the bowl of water. Close the door and bake for a further 10 minutes. To test if the loaf is done, turn it over and tap it on the base with your finger; if it sounds hollow it is ready. Place on a wire rack to cool.

BROWN SOURDOUGH LOAF

400g strong white flour

45g wholemeal flour

45g rye flour

140g Mother (see page 276)

320ml water (at 5°C)

80ml cold water (the bathe)

10g sea salt

Make as for the White Sourdough Loaf (see previous page). For a brown loaf, we finish it before baking by slashing four cuts on top, about 7cm long, to form a square.

RAISIN LOAF

110g raisins

110g currants

400g strong white flour

75g Mother (see page 276)

½ tsp fresh yeast

30g unsalted butter

220ml water (at 5°C)

8g sea salt

Fantastic with goat's or sheep's milk cheese. Both these cheeses have the amazing ability to make your last glass of wine taste as good as the first.

Soak the raisins and currants overnight in enough warm water just to cover.

MAKING THE DOUGH

Strain the raisins and currants, keeping the liquid. Place the flour, Mother, yeast and butter in an electric mixer and, using the dough hook attachment, mix on medium speed for 2 minutes just to break down the butter. Then add the water and mix on low speed for 4 minutes.

Use the soaking liquid from the dried fruit as the bathe; you will need 100ml, so top up with a little more water if necessary. Add a third of the bathe to begin with and mix the dough for 5 minutes on low speed. Add the next third and mix for 5 minutes. Add the final third and mix for 6 minutes. Leave the dough to rest for 20 minutes, then add the salt, currants and raisins and mix for a further 5 minutes.

RISING

Your dough will be very wet and hard to handle, so good luck, and remember – try not to add too much flour. Roll the dough into a ball, return it to the mixing bowl and sprinkle with flour. Cover with a cloth, place in the fridge and leave for 1 hour.

Remove the dough from the fridge and shape it into a ball again. Sprinkle with flour, cover and leave it somewhere warm (about 20°C, or warm room temperature) for about 3 hours, until it has risen a little.

Shape the dough into one large ball or split it in half to make two smaller loaves. Place on a baking tray and leave to rest for 15 minutes.

SHAPING

Shape the dough into a baton as best you can and place in a buttered large loaf tin. Sprinkle with flour, cover and leave for 2 hours or until the dough reaches the top of the tin.

BAKING

Preheat the oven to 210°C/Gas Mark 6½. Place a heatproof bowl of water on the bottom of the oven. This will produce steam, which will form a better crust.

Place the loaf in the oven and bake for 20 minutes. Open the oven door to let out any excess steam and remove the bowl of water. Carefully take the loaf out of the tin, lay it on its side on the oven shelf and bake for 5 minutes. Repeat on the other side, then remove from the oven and leave to cool on a wire rack.

SANDWICH LOAF

550g strong white flour
500g Old Dough (see page 278)
30g fresh yeast
15g sea salt
275ml water

This is not white sliced pap; this is a handsome, white, crusty beauty, which speaks cheese and chutney sandwich.

Place all the ingredients in an electric mixer and, using the dough hook attachment, mix on medium speed for 6–8 minutes. Cover the dough and leave to prove in the bowl for just 10 minutes. Then divide into 5 balls and place them in a buttered large loaf tin. Dust with flour and cover loosely with a cloth. Leave in a warm place for 1 hour, until doubled in size.

Place in an oven preheated to 220°C/Gas Mark 7 and bake for 20 minutes, then carefully remove the loaf from the tin, lay it on its side on the oven shelf and bake for a further 8 minutes. Repeat on the other side, then remove the loaf from the oven and leave to cool on a wire rack.

SODA BREAD

140g wholemeal self-raising flour

140g strong white flour

5g sea salt

10g caster sugar

5g baking powder

125ml water

125ml buttermilk

Fantastic toasted for breakfast with butter and Marmite.

Mix all the ingredients together by hand in a large mixing bowl (it will be quite wet), then leave the dough to rest in the bowl for 5 minutes.

Shape the dough into a ball and place on a floured baking tray. Sprinkle with flour and cut a cross in the top about 4cm long on each side and 1cm deep. Leave to rest for 10 minutes, then place in an oven preheated to 200°C/Gas Mark 6. Bake for 40 minutes, until golden brown. To test if the loaf is done, turn it over and tap it on the bottom with your finger; if it sounds hollow it is ready. Leave to cool on a wire rack. Serve with plenty of butter.

BAKING AND DOUGHNUTS

SEED CAKE AND A GLASS OF MADEIRA
LITTLE ANCHOVY BUNS
LITTLE CHOCOLATE BUNS
LITTLE PRUNE BUNS
TRENCHER
MADELEINES
PRUNE LOAF
SHORTBREAD
CRACKERS
THINS
KOLA KAKOR OR GOLDEN SYRUP BISCUITS
HAZELNUT BISCUITS
SPECULAAS
ST. JOHN ECCLES CAKES
DOUGHNUTS
CRÈME PÂTISSIÈRE
CHOCOLATE CUSTARD
LEMON CURD
RASPBERRY JAM
APPLE AND CINNAMON

SEED CAKE AND A GLASS OF MADEIRA

260g softened unsalted butter

260g caster sugar

1 tsp caraway seeds

5 large eggs, lightly beaten

320g self-raising flour

150ml full-fat milk

Eleven o'clock and still two hours until lunchtime. Something to keep you steady – nothing finer than a slice of seed cake, washed down with a glass of Madeira. This will see you safely through until lunch.

Grease a 16 x 10 x 8cm loaf tin with butter and line the base and sides with baking parchment.

Cream the butter, sugar and caraways together either with an electric mixer or in a bowl with a wooden spoon until they are white and fluffy. Gradually mix in the beaten eggs, adding them little by little to prevent curdling. Then sift in the flour and mix until incorporated. Lastly add the milk.

Transfer the mixture to the prepared tin and bake in an oven preheated to 180°C/Gas Mark 4 for 45 minutes or until it is golden brown and a skewer inserted in the centre comes out clean.

Serve with a glass of Madeira.

LITTLE ANCHOVY BUNS

Makes a dozen

210g strong white flour

90g Old Dough (see page 278)

35ml extra virgin olive oil

5g fresh yeast

55ml full-fat milk

1 tsp salt

65ml water

ANCHOVY PASTE

7 garlic cloves, peeled

a pinch of black pepper

1 tin of anchovies in oil, drained

up to 285ml extra virgin olive oil

a splash of red wine vinegar

In Florence there is a fantastic place with a wee slip of a bar, which offers little buns and a glass of white wine, just for those moments when you need some sustenance to keep you going in the day. Here is our take on the little steadying bun.

To make the anchovy paste, crush the garlic and pepper to a fine purée in a food processor or with a mortar and pestle, then add the anchovies and allow them to break down. Gradually add just enough oil to make a thick paste, then the vinegar to taste. Check the seasoning.

Place the flour, dough, oil, yeast, milk, salt and water in the bowl of an electric mixer and, with the dough hook, mix for 6–8 minutes, until smooth and elastic. Cover the dough and leave to prove for just 10 minutes. Then divide it into 12 balls and place on a floured baking tray. The buns will spread, so be sure to allow a little room between each one. Cover loosely with cling film and prove in a warm place for 2 hours.

Bake in an oven preheated to 200°C/Gas Mark 6 for 15 minutes, until the buns are golden brown. After baking, let them cool slightly, then slice them in half. Spread with the paste and sandwich them back together.

The anchovy paste can have many uses, depending on how thick you make it. With less oil and vinegar added, you will have a very firm paste, which is delicious spread on toast and eaten with sweet roasted shallots. If the full amount of oil is added, you will have a looser, though still emulsified, mixture, which is ideal for dressing boiled greens or broccoli – eat them on their own or with lamb or beef. It also makes an excellent dressing for bitter salad leaves.

LITTLE CHOCOLATE BUNS
Makes a dozen

210g strong white flour

90g Old Dough (see page 278)

35ml extra virgin olive oil

5g fresh yeast

55ml full-fat milk

1 tsp salt

65ml water

12 squares of dark chocolate, with at least 70 per cent cocoa solids

cocoa powder for dusting

There is nothing finer than warm little buttock-like buns.

Place the flour, dough, oil, yeast, milk, salt and water in the bowl of an electric mixer and, with the dough hook, mix for around 6–8 minutes, until smooth and elastic. Cover the dough and leave to prove for just 10 minutes. Then divide it into 12 balls and flatten out each one. Place a square of chocolate in the middle of the dough and pull the dough around it so it is completely enclosed. Reshape the dough into a ball and place on a floured baking tray. The buns will spread, so be sure to allow a little room between each one. Dust with cocoa powder, cover loosely with cling film and prove in a warm place for 2 hours.

Bake in an oven preheated to 200°C/Gas Mark 6 for 15 minutes, until the buns are golden brown. Serve immediately from the oven. Watch out, the filling will be like molten lava. Blow blow.

LITTLE PRUNE BUNS
Makes a dozen

Make these as for the chocolate version (see above), replacing the chocolate with 12 prunes and brushing the tops with beaten egg rather than dusting them with cocoa powder.

TRENCHER

Big enough for a large joint

110ml full-fat milk

60ml water

5g fresh yeast

275g strong white flour

5g caster sugar

5g salt

40g beef dripping

No finer thing than roast beef oozing into a trencher.

Heat the milk and water to blood temperature (37.5°C), then remove from the heat. Add the yeast and mix until dissolved. Leave in a warm place for about 10 minutes.

Sift the flour, sugar and salt into a bowl and rub in half the dripping. Add the yeast mixture and stir well to form a dough. Cover with a cloth and leave in a warm place for 10–15 minutes. Remove the dough from the bowl and knead on a floured work surface for 5 minutes, until smooth and elastic. Cover again and leave in a warm place for 25 minutes, until doubled in size.

Roll out the dough so it is a good 2–3cm bigger all round than your joint of meat. Place on a baking tray, cover and leave to prove for about 25 minutes, until doubled in size again. Bake in an oven preheated to 200°C/Gas Mark 6 for 20 minutes, until golden brown.

Slice the top off the trencher (just a thin slice) and discard it. Dot the rest of the dripping over the trencher and put it in the oven for just a few moments to melt. Place on a serving dish, pour some gravy over it and put the joint of meat on top. Then give the meat its normal resting time, so all the lovely juices get sucked into the trencher.

MADELEINES

Makes about two dozen

135g unsalted butter

2 tbsp pure honey

3 large eggs

110g caster sugar

15g soft light brown sugar

135g self-raising flour, sifted

Well, I feel Proust must have covered most aspects but what about a plate of warm madeleines in the afternoon with a bottle of pink champagne? Almost as good as elevenses.

You will need a madeleine tray.

Melt the butter and honey in a saucepan and simmer until golden brown. Leave to cool. Using an electric mixer, whisk the eggs, caster sugar and brown sugar together for 8–10 minutes, until the mixture has tripled in volume and leaves a trail on the surface for a few seconds when the whisk is lifted.

Fold the sifted flour and melted butter through the egg mixture until it is all incorporated. Pour into a plastic container and leave to rest in the fridge for 2–3 hours.

Grease the madeleine moulds with butter, then dust them with flour, tapping off any excess. Place a dessertspoon of the mixture in each mould and bake in an oven preheated to 190°C/Gas Mark 5 for 12–15 minutes, until firm to the touch and golden brown.

PRUNE LOAF

125g softened unsalted butter

110g soft light brown sugar

3 large eggs, lightly beaten

225g plain flour

1 tsp bicarbonate of soda

2 tbsp vanilla extract

4 tbsp black treacle

3 tbsp prune juice

3 tbsp full-fat milk

600g tea-soaked prunes
(see page 322)

MIST

75ml prune juice

25ml Vieille Prune

Onomatopoeically a joy.

Grease a 30 x 11 x 7cm loaf tin with butter and line the base and sides with baking parchment.

Cream the butter and sugar together either with an electric mixer or in a bowl with a wooden spoon until they are white and fluffy. Gradually beat in the eggs, adding them little by little to prevent curdling. Sift in the flour and bicarbonate of soda and mix in. Then add the vanilla extract, black treacle, prune juice and milk. This should leave you with a fairly wet mixture.

Fill the lined loaf tin just over halfway with the mixture. Place the prunes on top, patting them down gently, but not all the way to the bottom, so they're evenly distributed. Chill in the fridge for 2 hours. This stops the prunes sinking to the bottom of the loaf.

Bake in an oven preheated to 180°C/Gas Mark 4 for 45–50 minutes, until a skewer inserted into the middle of the loaf comes out clean. Remove from the oven, place on a cooling rack and leave for 10 minutes before serving.

Now for the mist: heat the prune juice in a small saucepan until it starts to boil, then add the Vieille Prune and take it off the heat. Serve the loaf warm, with Vanilla Ice Cream (see page 382) or extra-thick Jersey cream, and pour 2 tablespoons of mist over each serving.

SHORTBREAD

Makes twenty to thirty biscuits, enough to fill your biscuit tin right to the top

750g plain flour

500g cold unsalted butter, cut into small cubes

250g caster sugar

Shortbread is rather like Lutyens' Castle Drogo, which he built with three ingredients: wood, glass and stone. Both are splendid.

Sift the flour into a large bowl, add the butter and rub them together with your fingertips. What you are looking for is a breadcrumb consistency; when you reach that stage, add the sugar and rub it in until you have a smooth paste. It will be a little crumbly but that comes from the shortness of the mix. Wrap the dough in cling film and let it rest in the fridge for about 30 minutes.

Roll out on a lightly floured surface to about 8mm thick and then cut into rounds with a 3cm pastry cutter. Place on baking trays lined with baking parchment and bake in an oven preheated to 160°C/Gas Mark 3 for about 10–15 minutes. The shortbread should be very pale, so be careful not to overcook it.

CRACKERS

These quantities make plenty; they will keep in a tin

1.125kg strong white flour

2 tsp baking powder

1 tsp poppy seeds

1 tsp dill seeds

1 tsp caraway seeds

2 tsp sea salt

175ml extra virgin olive oil

about 400ml cold water

Excellent biscuits to eat with cheese.

Sift the flour and baking powder together, then mix all the dry ingredients together. Add the extra virgin olive oil, stir this in, then cautiously add the water: you want a fairly soft dough, but not sticky. The dough is now ready to use.

On a large flat table sprinkle some flour and dust your rolling pin, roll out the dough to a thickness of approximately 5mm, then cut into your biscuits' chosen shape. May I suggest a round with a 5cm diameter? The dough left can be kneaded together and rolled out again. Roll the cut shapes out again as thin as you can, place onto a clean baking tray, then into a medium to hot oven, and bake for 10 minutes, keeping a close eye on them so as to avoid burning (don't worry if you do burn them, you are not alone; somehow fate has it that one burns biscuits, so bake them in batches).

Allow to cool on a rack. Eat or store in an airtight container.

THINS

Makes lots; but the raw dough keeps very well in the freezer

450g unsalted butter

450g caster sugar, plus extra
for sprinkling

2 large eggs

580g plain flour, sifted

a pinch of salt

2 tsp baking powder

1 tsp vanilla extract

*ONE OF THE FOLLOWING
FLAVOURINGS*

3–4 tsp ground cinnamon
or ginger

2–3 tsp grated orange or
lemon zest

1–2 tsp liquid malt

It's strange how the word thins gets one going.

Cream the butter and sugar together until light and fluffy, then beat in the eggs one at a time. Beat in the sifted flour, salt, baking powder, vanilla extract and your chosen flavouring. Shape the dough into a log about 20 x 2 x 8cm, wrap in cling film and chill for about 30 minutes, until firm.

Slice the log as thinly as you can (that's why they are Thins, not Thicks) and place on a baking sheet lined with baking parchment (you can just slice off as many as you need, then wrap the remaining dough and keep it in the fridge or freezer). Bake in an oven preheated to 160°C/Gas Mark 3 for 5–8 minutes, until golden brown. Remove from the oven, sprinkle with caster sugar and leave to cool.

KOLA KAKOR OR GOLDEN SYRUP BISCUITS

Makes forty

360g plain flour

2 tsp baking powder

1 vanilla pod

200g soft unsalted butter, diced

200g caster sugar

90g golden syrup

Comfort itself. This recipe comes from Therese, one of the pastry chefs at St. John, and yes, she is from Sweden.

Sift the flour and baking powder into a bowl. Slit the vanilla pod lengthways, scrape out the seeds and mix them into the flour. Add all the rest of the ingredients and mix well until you have a firm, smooth paste – this can be done by hand or in a food mixer fitted with the beater attachment.

Divide the mixture into 4 pieces and roll out each one to 25cm long and 2.5cm thick. Place on a baking tray lined with baking parchment, making sure they are at least 10cm apart as they will spread out in the oven (best to do 2 rolls per baking tray). Bake at 180°C/Gas Mark 4 for 25–30 minutes, until golden brown. When they come out of the oven, leave for 2 minutes, then cut each piece into 10 strips. Great served with ice cream, cream desserts or just a mug of tea.

HAZELNUT BISCUITS
Makes lots

140g unsalted butter

140g caster sugar

1 large egg yolk

140g plain flour

280g whole roasted hazelnuts

Perfect to serve with Bitter Chocolate Cream (see page 324).

Using an electric mixer, cream the butter and sugar together until white and fluffy, then beat in the egg yolk. Mix in the flour, followed by the roasted hazelnuts. Mix on full speed for 2–4 minutes to break down the hazelnuts a little. Remove the dough from the mixing bowl and roll it into a log about 3cm in diameter. Wrap in cling film and chill for 1–2 hours.

Cut the log into slices 5mm thick and place on a baking sheet lined with baking parchment. The biscuits will spread, so be sure to leave a little room between each one. Bake in an oven preheated to 160°C/Gas Mark 3 for 10 minutes or until golden.

SPECULAAS

Makes fifteen to twenty

125g unsalted butter

150g Demerara sugar

grated zest of 1 lemon

250g plain flour

½ tsp baking powder

a pinch of salt

30g flaked almonds

10g mixed candied peel, finely chopped

100ml full-fat milk

SPICE MIX

2 tbsp ground cinnamon

2 tsp ground nutmeg

2 tsp ground cloves

2 tsp ground mace

2 tsp ground ginger

Great name, great biscuit.

Mix together all the ingredients for the spice mix (you won't need it all for this recipe but it will keep well in a tightly sealed jar).

Cream the butter, sugar and lemon zest together for 3–4 minutes. The mixture will not go light and fluffy because of the coarse grains of the sugar but creaming it will bring out the flavour of the lemon. Sift in the flour, baking powder, salt and 3 teaspoons of the spice mix and fold them in. It won't form a dough because the liquid has not been added yet. Now stir in the flaked almonds and mixed peel. Lastly stir in the milk to form a dough. Shape it into a log about 3cm thick, wrap in cling film and chill for 1–2 hours.

Cut the dough into slices about 4mm thick and place them on a baking tray lined with baking parchment. The biscuits will spread, so leave a little room between each one. Bake in an oven preheated to 160°C/Gas Mark 3 for 10–15 minutes, until golden brown.

ST. JOHN ECCLES CAKES

Should easily make a dozen cakes – if you have pastry left over it freezes very well

50g unsalted butter
110g dark brown sugar
220g currants
1 tsp ground allspice
1 tsp ground nutmeg
Puff Pastry (see page 231)
3 egg whites, beaten with a fork
a shallow bowl of caster sugar

I stress the *St. John* in our Eccles cake, as I am sure Eccles cake bakers in Eccles will not recognize them as an Eccles cake they know.

Oddly enough, for a restaurant with a certain carnivorous reputation, we serve a vegetarian Eccles cake, omitting to use the traditional lard in the pastry; instead we use puff pastry, so apologies to Eccles, but this recipe's results are delicious and particularly fine when consumed with Lancashire cheese.

To make the filling, melt the butter and sugar together, then add them to the dry ingredients, mix well, and then leave to cool before using.

Roll the puff pastry out to 8mm thick and cut circles approximately 9cm in diameter. Onto these spoon a blob of your filling mixture in the centre of the circle, and pull up the sides of the pastry to cover the filling. Seal it with your fingers, then turn it over and slash the top. Paint the top with the egg white, then dip it into the sugar. The Eccles cakes are now ready to bake for 15 to 20 minutes in a hot to medium oven; keep an eye on them so that they don't burn. They can be eaten hot or cold and, as I mentioned earlier, are particularly marvellous when eaten with Lancashire cheese.

The reason we slash the top of the Eccles cake three times is for the Holy Trinity (well, that's what I have been told).

DOUGHNUTS

Makes twenty-five

500g strong white flour

65g caster sugar, plus extra
for coating

10g salt

15g fresh yeast

4 large eggs

grated zest of 1 lemon

155ml water

125g softened unsalted butter

sunflower oil for deep-frying

I've tried eating Justin's doughnuts without licking my lips. I was doing well, then the custard spurted onto my glasses – that was the moment when loss of concentration led to lip licking.

A weakness for custard aside, all Justin's doughnuts have the *licko lip* factor.

You will need a freestanding electric mixer fitted with the beater attachment.

Place all the ingredients except the butter and oil in the bowl of the mixer. Mix together on medium speed for 6 minutes, then scrape down the sides of the bowl. Start mixing on medium speed again, adding the soft butter about 20g at a time until all of it is incorporated. Keep mixing for 6–8 minutes, until the dough has come away from the sides of the bowl and looks smooth, glossy and elastic.

Place the dough in a large bowl, sprinkle the surface with flour and cover the bowl with a tea towel. Leave to rise for 2–3 hours in a warm place, until doubled in size, then knock back the dough. Cover the bowl with cling film and place in the fridge for at least 4 hours or overnight.

Cut the dough into 25 pieces and roll them into smooth balls. Place on floured baking sheets, leaving about 5cm between each one. Cover with cling film and leave to prove for 2–3 hours, depending on how warm it is; they should double in size.

Half fill a deep-fat fryer or a deep, heavy-based saucepan with sunflower oil and heat it to 190°C. The temperature is very important: too high and the doughnuts will burn; too low and they will absorb the oil, making them greasy.

With the oil at the right temperature, start frying the doughnuts, in batches of 3 or 4 at a time, until golden brown. They will take about 2 minutes on each side. Remember to check the temperature of the oil between each batch. As the doughnuts are done, place them on kitchen paper to soak up excess oil and then toss in caster sugar.

The doughnuts are fantastic on their own but on Sundays we sell them at the bakery at St. John Bread & Wine filled with crème pâtissière, lemon curd, chocolate custard, apple and cinnamon and homemade jam. So the next five recipes are for doughnut fillings and their possibilities.

If you decide to fill your doughnuts, you will need a piping bag with a nozzle. Make a hole in each doughnut with a small knife and pipe in the filling. We fill them very generously – about 4 tablespoons of filling per doughnut.

CRÈME PÂTISSIÈRE

Makes enough to fill twenty-five doughnuts

2 vanilla pods

1 litre full-fat milk

12 large egg yolks

130g caster sugar

80g plain flour

250ml lightly whipped double cream (optional)

Slit the vanilla pods lengthways and scrape out the seeds. Put the pods and seeds in a saucepan with the milk and bring to the boil over a medium heat.

Meanwhile, mix the egg yolks and sugar together in a large bowl. Sift in the flour and whisk all together. When the milk is boiling, pour it over the egg mixture, whisking all the time. Then return the mixture to the saucepan and slowly bring to the boil over a low heat, whisking occasionally. Once it is boiling, whisk continuously for about 5 minutes, until very thick and smooth. Strain through a fine sieve into a bowl and cover the surface with cling film to prevent a skin forming. Leave to cool, then chill. (Keep the vanilla pods; if you wash them out, dry them in a low oven and store in a jar of caster sugar; you will have some lovely vanilla sugar in a month or two.)

If using the crème pâtissière for doughnuts, lighten it up by folding the whipped cream into it.

CRÈME PÂTISSIÈRE: ITS POSSIBILITIES
Custard slice
Tarts
Pancakes
Mousses
Profiteroles

CHOCOLATE CUSTARD

Makes enough to fill twenty-five doughnuts

1 litre full-fat milk

12 large egg yolks

130g caster sugar

65g plain flour

200g plain chocolate, with at least 70 per cent cocoa solids, finely chopped

250ml lightly whipped double cream (optional)

Pour the milk into a saucepan and bring to the boil over a medium heat. Meanwhile, mix the egg yolks and sugar together in a large bowl. Sift in the flour and whisk all together. When the milk is boiling, pour it over the egg mixture, whisking all the time. Then return the mixture to the saucepan and slowly bring to the boil over a low heat, whisking occasionally.

Once it is boiling, whisk continuously for about 5 minutes, until very thick and smooth. Strain through a fine sieve into a heatproof bowl. Add the chocolate and whisk it into the hot custard until dissolved. Cover the surface with cling film to prevent a skin forming, leave to cool, then chill.

If using the chocolate custard for doughnuts, we like to lighten it up by folding the whipped cream into it.

CHOCOLATE CUSTARD: ITS POSSIBILITIES

Black Forest trifle

Pancakes

Tarts

Profiteroles

Chocolate cake

Custard slice

LEMON CURD

Makes two jars

juice and finely grated zest of 6 lemons

200g unsalted butter, cut into small cubes

410g caster sugar

6 large eggs, lightly beaten

Place the lemon juice and zest in a large heatproof bowl with the butter and sugar. Set the bowl over a saucepan of simmering water, making sure the water doesn't touch the base of the bowl. Leave until the butter has melted, stirring occasionally, then whisk in the beaten eggs. Cook for about 10 minutes, whisking every 2–3 minutes, until the lemon curd has thickened. Watch the simmering water to make sure it doesn't boil rapidly or the eggs will curdle. Once the curd has thickened, strain it through a fine sieve, then pot in sterilized jars and seal. It will keep for up to 3 months in the fridge.

TO STERILIZE JARS

Put some clamp-top preserving jars through a dishwasher cycle a couple of times. Place the lemon curd (or jam or mincemeat) in the jars and seal, then put the jars into a large, deep saucepan. Cover with water, bring to the boil and simmer for 15–20 minutes for a 450g jar, topping up the water if necessary.

LEMON CURD: ITS POSSIBILITIES

Pancakes

Ice cream

Lemon meringue pie

Sponge cakes

Tart

Profiteroles

Steamed puddings

Toast

RASPBERRY JAM

Makes two to three jars

900g jam sugar

1kg raspberries

juice of 2 lemons

Place the sugar in a roasting tin and warm gently in a low oven (about 140°C/Gas Mark 1) for 20 minutes. Meanwhile, place the raspberries and lemon juice in a large, heavy-based saucepan and bring to the boil over a low heat. Add the sugar and stir until dissolved. Simmer for 10–15 minutes or until setting point is reached. To test for setting point, place a plate in the fridge until cold, then place a small spoonful of jam on it. If you draw your finger through the jam, it should remain separated and not run back into the centre.

As soon as the jam reaches setting point, spoon it into sterilized jars (see previous page) and seal.

RASPBERRY JAM: ITS POSSIBILITIES
Pancakes
Tarts
Toast
Sponge cakes
Queen of puddings
Ripple ice cream

APPLE AND CINNAMON
Makes enough to fill twenty-five doughnuts

*8 large Bramley apples, peeled,
cored and cut into small pieces*

200g soft light brown sugar

50ml water

1 cinnamon stick

*juice and finely grated
zest of 1 lemon*

2 tsp ground cinnamon (optional)

Place the apples, sugar, water and cinnamon stick in a saucepan and set it over a low heat. Cook for 5 minutes, then add the lemon juice and zest. Cook for another 25 minutes, stirring occasionally, until the apples have collapsed into a purée.

If you are using the mixture to fill doughnuts, add the ground cinnamon to the sugar for dusting the doughnuts after frying them.

APPLE AND CINNAMON: ITS POSSIBILITIES
Pancakes
Ripple ice cream
Trifle
Tarts
Sponge cakes
Granola and yoghurt

PUDDINGS

STORE CUPBOARD
HOT CHOCOLATE PUDDING
BITTER CHOCOLATE CREAM
PROFITEROLES STUFFED WITH VANILLA ICE CREAM
CHOCOLATE BAKED ALASKA
ABBEY'S CHOCOLATE CAKE WITH CHOCOLATE CARAMEL SAUCE
DAMSON JELLY
TOM'S CHERRY TRIFLE
APPLE AND CALVADOS TRIFLE
SUMMER PUDDING
BLACK HAT
QUINCE AND PRUNES
CARRAGHEEN PUDDING
YOU FOOL
GINGER LOAF
RHUBARB CRUMBLE CAKE
BAKED GOAT'S CURD CHEESECAKE
BURNT SHEEP'S MILK YOGHURT
GOAT'S CURD AND MARC
TREACLE TART
CUSTARD TART
QUEEN OF PUDDINGS
RICE PUDDING WITH MARC AND RAISIN CUSTARD

STORE CUPBOARD

Prepare these at least two weeks before use; they will keep for ages.

A jar of Agen prunes covered in Earl Grey tea (just fill your jar with prunes, add a couple of Earl Grey teabags and a few strips of lemon zest, then cover with boiling water and seal the jar).

A jar of sultanas or raisins covered in marc (fill a jar with sultanas or raisins, top up with marc and seal).

HOT CHOCOLATE PUDDING

To serve eight

250g plain chocolate, with at least 70 per cent cocoa solids, cut into small chunks

250g unsalted butter, diced, plus extra for greasing

6 large eggs

5 large egg yolks

125g caster sugar, plus extra for dusting

75g plain flour

Here is a pudding that needs no introduction.

Grease 8 individual ramekins or dariole moulds (or one large ovenproof dish) with butter and dust with caster sugar.

Put the chocolate and butter in a heatproof bowl and place over a saucepan of simmering water, making sure the water doesn't touch the base of the bowl. Leave until melted. Meanwhile, using an electric mixer on full speed, whisk the eggs, yolks and sugar together for about 6 minutes, until they have at least tripled in volume.

Sift the flour into a bowl and slowly pour on the melted chocolate and butter mixture, whisking constantly until a thin paste has formed. Fold this into the whisked egg mixture very carefully but quickly, as the chocolate will start to set. Pour into the prepared dishes and bake in an oven preheated to 180°C/Gas Mark 4, until risen and firm on the outside but soft in the centre. The large one will take about 30 minutes to cook, the individual ones about 13 minutes.

Serve with crème fraîche or ice cream and, if in season, some cherries.

BITTER CHOCOLATE CREAM

To serve six

250g plain chocolate, with at least
70 per cent cocoa solids (we use an
El Rey Venezuelan chocolate called
Apamate, at 73.5 per cent)

1 gelatine leaf

375ml double cream

125ml full-fat milk

100g caster sugar

Cor blimey!

Cut the chocolate into small chunks, put it in a large bowl and set aside. Put the gelatine leaf in a separate bowl and cover with cold water.

Pour the cream and milk into a saucepan, add the caster sugar and bring slowly to the boil, whisking occasionally. Now go back to your gelatine and squeeze out the water. Once the cream is boiling, take it off the heat, add the squeezed-out gelatine leaf and whisk until dissolved. Then strain the hot cream mixture over the chocolate and whisk until the chocolate has dissolved. You will have a beautiful, glossy chocolate cream.

Pour the mixture into 6 individual moulds or one large serving dish and leave in the fridge for 4–6 hours, until set. Serve with Hazelnut Biscuits (see page 308) and tea-soaked prunes (see page 322), or with cherries when in season.

PROFITEROLES STUFFED WITH VANILLA ICE CREAM

To serve eight

250ml water

100g unsalted butter, diced

140g strong white flour

a pinch of salt

2 tsp caster sugar

5 large eggs, lightly beaten

Vanilla Ice Cream (see page 382)

HOT CHOCOLATE SAUCE

500g plain chocolate, with at least 70 per cent cocoa solids, broken into chunks

700ml water

120g caster sugar

Vanilla ice cream and chocolate sauce are a match made in heaven, but then add the rigour of the pastry …

Place the water and butter in a deep, heavy-based saucepan and bring to the boil – do this slowly, so the butter will just have melted by the time the water is boiling. Remove from the heat and immediately stir in the flour, salt and sugar. Return the pan to a medium heat and beat with a wooden spoon until the mixture becomes smooth and no longer sticks to the sides of the pan. Leave to cool for 3–4 minutes, then gradually beat in the eggs one at a time, until the mixture is shiny and thick enough to drop reluctantly from the spoon. Cover with cling film and leave to cool.

Line a baking sheet with baking parchment. Fill a piping bag with the mixture and pipe it onto the baking tray in balls 1.5cm in diameter. The profiteroles will spread, so be sure to allow a little room between each one.

Bake in an oven preheated to 220°C/Gas Mark 7 for 20–25 minutes, until crisp and golden brown. Remove from the oven and leave to cool on a wire rack.

For the hot chocolate sauce, place all the ingredients in a heavy-based saucepan and bring slowly to the boil. Pass through a fine sieve.

To serve, slice the profiteroles widthways through the middle and fill with vanilla ice cream. Serve with a jug of piping-hot chocolate sauce.

CHOCOLATE BAKED ALASKA

To serve eight

a splash of good brandy

Chocolate Ice Cream (see page 387)

GÉNOISE SPONGE

4 large eggs

125g caster sugar

125g plain flour, sifted

50g unsalted butter, melted

MERINGUE

3 large egg whites

240g caster sugar

With much research into chocolate ice cream, we had plenty of the stuff around, hence the Chocolate Baked Alaska. What could be finer than the white, fluffy exterior surrounding the dark middle?

First make the génoise sponge. Using an electric mixer, whisk the eggs and caster sugar on full speed for about 5 minutes, until tripled in volume. Fold the sifted flour through the mixture with a large metal spoon until completely incorporated, then fold in the melted butter. Pour into a parchment-lined 16 x 23cm baking tray, about 2.5cm deep, and place in an oven preheated to 160°C/Gas Mark 3. Bake for 25 minutes or until the sponge is firm to the touch and golden brown. Turn out onto a wire rack to cool.

Cut a circle out of the sponge about 20cm in diameter. Place it on a baking tray lined with baking parchment, then pour the brandy over it and leave for 1 hour.

Now make the meringue. Make sure your bowl and whisk are very clean before you start. Whisk the egg whites until they form stiff peaks, then gradually add the sugar, whisking until stiff and glossy.

Remove the chocolate ice cream from the freezer and pile it up on the sponge, leaving a 2.5cm border all round. Cover the whole Alaska with the meringue, starting from the rim of the sponge, then moving up over the ice cream. Place the Alaska in an oven preheated to 220°C/Gas Mark 7 for 8–10 minutes, until the meringue is golden brown. If you're worried the ice cream might be about to melt before the meringue is well coloured, insert a skewer and check that it comes out cold. Serve right away, with thick cream.

ABBEY'S CHOCOLATE CAKE WITH CHOCOLATE CARAMEL SAUCE

To serve twelve to sixteen

360g unsalted butter,
cut into small cubes

440g plain chocolate, with
70 per cent cocoa solids,
finely chopped

550g caster sugar

200g ground almonds

125g cocoa powder

10 eggs, lightly beaten

a pinch of salt

CHOCOLATE CARAMEL
SAUCE

310g caster sugar

375ml double cream

300g plain chocolate, with
70 per cent cocoa solids,
finely chopped

a pinch of salt

Abbey used to work at St. John Bread & Wine. We now use her chocolate cake recipe at both restaurants. So it's all your fault, Abbey!

Put the butter and chocolate in a bowl and place over a pan of simmering water, making sure the water isn't touching the base of the bowl. Melt together, whisking occasionally, then take off the heat. Stir in the sugar.

Sift the ground almonds (you might be left with a few that won't go through but that is fine, you can use them in something else), then mix them with the cocoa powder. Add to the chocolate mix, mix well, then stir in the eggs and salt and mix again.

Pour the mixture into a 25cm cake tin (about 8cm deep) lined with baking parchment. Bake at 160°C/Gas Mark 3 for around 35 minutes; the middle will still be slightly uncooked but it will set in the residual heat. Remove from the oven and leave to cool.

To make the sauce, place the sugar in a large, deep, heavy-based saucepan with a couple of tablespoons of water and let it melt over a medium heat. Raise the heat and cook without stirring until it turns into a dark brown caramel. Then slowly add the cream – watch out, it will spit a little – and turn the heat down low. Let the caramel melt into the cream, whisking occasionally, then remove from the heat and add the chocolate and salt, whisking until the chocolate has dissolved. Pass through a fine sieve into a bowl. If you want to warm the sauce up, best to do it over a pan of simmering water.

Serve the cake with the sauce and some crème fraîche or Vanilla Ice Cream (see page 382).

DAMSON JELLY

To serve four

500g damsons

100ml water

125g caster sugar

leaf gelatine

Jelly doesn't fail to please. No one can resist that wobble.

Place the damsons in a heavy-based saucepan, add the water and sugar and bring to the boil, stirring to dissolve the sugar. Simmer gently until the damsons are soft. (You can also do this in the oven in a deep roasting tin but bring the water and sugar to the boil first and pour them over the damsons. Cover with foil and bake at 160°C/Gas Mark 3.)

Let the damsons cool and then leave in the fridge for 2 days; this seems a long time but it produces a really well-flavoured juice.

After 2 days, strain the juice from the damsons, set the damsons aside and measure the juice; you should have about 600ml, for which you will need 3 gelatine leaves. Soak the gelatine leaves in cold water for about 8 minutes. Meanwhile, heat 300ml of the damson juice until hot. Squeeze the water out of the gelatine leaves, add them to the hot damson juice and whisk until dissolved. Then whisk into the rest of the juice and pour through a fine sieve into a jelly mould. Leave in the fridge overnight to set.

Serve with some of the poached damsons, plus whipped cream and Madeleines (see page 301).

POACHED DAMSONS: THEIR POSSIBILITIES
Hot with vanilla ice cream
Crumbles
Tarts
Yoghurt and granola
Fool
Ripple ice cream

TOM'S CHERRY TRIFLE
Makes six individual portions

For this recipe I leave you in the capable hands of Tom …

The individual recipe components should ideally be made the day before the pudding is to be served. Also, this trifle doesn't really work when done as one large bowlful because, unlike my mother's, the fruit isn't set in a jelly but in a thick compote and so remains a little runny.

CUSTARD
Place the milk, cream and vanilla pod in a saucepan and bring to the boil. In a large round-bottomed bowl whisk the yolks with the sugar until smooth.

When the milk and cream have boiled pour them onto the yolks and whisk until thoroughly blended. Return to the pan and stir with a wooden spoon. Cook over a gentle heat until the custard coats the back of the spoon. Whatever you do, do not let the custard boil or it will split and be unusable. Pass through a fine sieve and set aside to cool.

TRIFLE SPONGES
Place the yolks in a mixing bowl and add half the sugar. Whisk by hand or with an electric mixer until light and fluffy. In a separate clean bowl whisk the whites until they form soft peaks, then, as you continue to whisk, slowly add the remaining sugar. Sift together the flour and cornflour and cover a baking sheet with silicon or greaseproof paper.

Now begin folding the mixture together. Fold one-third of the egg white and one-third of the flour into the yolks and repeat until all the mixtures are combined.

You can either pipe the mixture onto the baking sheet in traditional finger shapes or (much easier) spread it evenly on the tray. Either way dust the mix with icing sugar and place in a warm to medium oven for approximately 15 minutes, but keep a close eye on it. When lightly golden remove from the oven and leave to cool. This recipe is probably more than ample for the trifle but the biscuits keep for weeks if stored in an airtight tin.

CHERRY COMPOTE

Place the sugar in the bottom of a small stainless-steel pan, and dissolve it with a little water, making sure that the sides of the pan are clean and free of sugar crystals. Place over a gentle heat. The sugar needs to be boiled until it thickens to a dense syrup: if you have a sugar thermometer it's the soft ball point; if you haven't, look for a glucose consistency with large bubbles. When the sugar reaches this point throw in 115g of the cherries and the lemon juice and stir well. Turn down the heat and let the cherries stew for 10 minutes.

Carefully pour the mixture into a blender and purée. While hot pour the mixture onto the remaining fruit, cover and leave to steep and soften. When all your ingredients are cool you can assemble the trifle.

ASSEMBLING THE TRIFLE

Divide the cherry mixture between six ramekins but do not fill any more than one-third full. Next place a layer of diced trifle sponge and soak with medium sherry or, if you feel a little extravagant, Marsala wine, and allow to seep in for 10 minutes or so. Press down and pour over the custard, ideally leaving a little space at the top of the ramekin.

Place in the fridge overnight but remove 30 minutes before it is to be served. To finish, spoon over some crème fraîche or, to be utterly sinful, a dollop of Jersey cream, and a sprinkling of toasted almonds.

APPLE AND CALVADOS TRIFLE

To serve six to eight

3 large Bramley apples, peeled, cored and roughly chopped

3 Cox apples, peeled, cored and roughly chopped

2 tbsp soft light brown sugar

½ tsp ground cinnamon

at least 6 tbsp Calvados

SPONGE

4 large eggs

125g caster sugar

125g plain flour, sifted

CUSTARD

450ml double cream

1 tsp vanilla extract

2 large eggs

2 large egg yolks

85g caster sugar

ALMONDS

100g flaked almonds

30g icing sugar

1 tbsp Calvados

CREAM

300ml double cream

30g icing sugar

1 tsp vanilla extract

Gone are the hundreds and thousands, the boring jelly, the tinned fruit. Trifle has found its perch again.

First prepare the sponge. Whisk the eggs and sugar on high speed with an electric mixer for 3–4 minutes, until tripled in volume. Slowly fold in the sifted flour, then pour into a Swiss roll tin lined with baking parchment. Place in an oven preheated to 160°C/Gas Mark 3 and bake for about 25 minutes, until golden brown and firm to the touch. Turn out onto a wire rack to cool.

Place the Bramleys and Coxes apples in a saucepan with the sugar and cinnamon. Cook over a medium heat until the apples are tender, then set aside to cool.

To make the custard, pour the double cream and vanilla extract into a saucepan and bring to the boil. Meanwhile, mix the eggs, egg yolks and sugar together in a large bowl. Once the cream reaches boiling point, pour it over the egg mixture, whisking constantly to prevent the eggs scrambling. Strain through a fine sieve into a large heatproof bowl, then place the bowl over a pan of simmering water. Whisk occasionally until the custard has thickened. Pour through a fine sieve into a plastic container, leave to cool, then chill.

Mix the almonds, icing sugar and Calvados together in a bowl, then spread them out on a baking tray. Toast in an oven preheated to 180°C/Gas Mark 4 for 6–8 minutes, until golden brown.

For the cream, whisk the double cream, icing sugar and vanilla extract together until soft peaks are formed, then place in the fridge.

To assemble the trifle, you will need a large glass bowl. Cut the sponge into slices 2cm thick (nothing worse than not enough booze-soaked sponge) and place in the bottom of your bowl. Then pour on at least 6 tablespoons of Calvados and leave for 30 minutes to soak in. Cover with the apple mixture, then the thick custard, then the cream. Each layer should be roughly the same thickness. Top with the sugared roasted almonds.

SUMMER PUDDING

To serve six to eight

250g caster sugar

1 litre water

250g strawberries

250g raspberries

250g redcurrants

1 Sandwich Loaf
(see page 289)

I am not a fan of individual summer puddings, as there is always too much bread and not enough fruit. That's why we make our summer puddings to serve at least two.

Put the sugar and water in a large saucepan and bring to the boil, stirring to dissolve the sugar. Simmer for 5 minutes. Add the strawberries, bring back to a simmer, then take off the heat and add the raspberries and redcurrants. Pour the mixture into a plastic container and leave to cool, then place in the fridge overnight (leaving it this long means that plenty of juices will leach out of the fruit).

Line a 2.3 litre pudding basin with cling film, leaving plenty overhanging. Cut the crusts off the bread and slice it about 8mm thick. Use the bread to line the sides of the basin, squeezing the slices in so there are no gaps. Then cut a disc to cover the bottom of the basin and a larger disc that will fit the top. Place the small disc in the basin and pour the fruit into it, filling it right to the top and including as much juice as possible. Place the larger disc of bread on top, pull up the excess cling film to seal all the juices in and tie the ends in a knot. Return any leftover fruit or juice to the fridge.

Put the basin in a deep plastic tray and weight the pudding down by placing a flat tray on it and then putting something heavy on top of that – tins of food will do nicely. Then leave overnight in the fridge.

To serve, turn the pudding out onto a large serving dish and pour some of the remaining juice over it. Accompany with a bowl of extra-thick Jersey cream.

YOU CAN SERVE ANY LEFTOVER FRUIT WITH:
Meringues and cream
Yoghurt and granola
Custard

Or turn it into a fool

YOU CAN TURN ANY LEFTOVER JUICE INTO:
Jellies
Ices

Or add a few drops to a glass of champagne

BLACK HAT

To serve six to eight

The Black Hat is basically an autumnal summer pudding, so the rules about size still apply.

Make as for Summer Pudding (see previous page) but increase the amount of sugar to 320g, replace the strawberries with 250g plums (stoned), and the other fruit with 250g blackberries, 250g blackcurrants and 100g elderberries.

QUINCE AND PRUNES

To serve four

2 litres water

500g caster sugar

6 large quinces

12 prunes (Agen, if possible)

I think it is vital to get prunes with their stones in, which gives them structure to swell with joy but maintain their prune dignity.

Place the water and sugar in a saucepan and bring to the boil, stirring occasionally to help the sugar to dissolve.

Meanwhile, peel the quinces but keep the skin and put to one side. Cut the quinces into quarters, remove the cores and keep these also. Lay the peel and cores in a large, deep roasting dish (their pigment turns the quinces that lovely ruby colour), cover with a sheet of baking parchment, then put the quinces on top.

When the water and sugar mixture comes to the boil, pour it over the quinces and cover with baking parchment. Weight down with a couple of heavy plates, then cover with foil. Place in an oven preheated to 140°C/Gas Mark 1 and bake for 4–5 hours, until the quinces are soft. Remove the foil, plates and parchment, add the prunes, then cover with foil again and leave to cool.

Serve hot, with either pouring cream or Vanilla Ice Cream (see page 382). They're also great just on their own.

QUINCE AND PRUNES: THEIR POSSIBILITIES
Jellies, with all that juice (remember, 3 leaves of gelatine per 600ml)
Crumbles
Tarts
Strudel (cheers, Lee)
Pies

CARRAGHEEN PUDDING

To serve six

225g carragheen

1.1 litres milk

caster sugar

*thick cream and good
jam to accompany*

Carragheen is a seaweed found in the Hebrides and Ireland. If you're not in either of these places picking from the shore, there's a good chance your local health-food shop will have it.

Put the carragheen, milk and sugar into a pan, and bring to a gentle simmer, stirring occasionally, for about 20 minutes, by which time the carragheen will appear to have half melted. Strain the liquid, discarding the remains of the seaweed, into a bowl and put in the fridge to set. It should turn out with ease.

This may sound like a very dour milk pudding, but let me assure you the carragheen gives the dish many particular qualities, some of which are hard to put one's finger on.

In its purity it goes very well with very thick, rich cream and a blob of good jam.

YOU FOOL

To serve two

200g *blackberries
or any fruit you desire*

50g *caster sugar*

400ml *double cream*

Who are you calling a fool?

Put the fruit in a pan with half the sugar and cook very gently for a few minutes (if you use tart fruit such as rhubarb, you will need more sugar). All you are looking to do with the fruit is soften it until the juices start to run. If the fruit is really ripe you won't even need to cook it – just mix it with the sugar and crush lightly with a fork.

Leave the fruit to cool. Whip the cream with the rest of the sugar until it forms soft peaks, then fold in the fruit. Serve with Shortbread (see page 303).

GINGER LOAF
To serve eight to ten

300g self-raising flour

1½ tbsp ground ginger

1 tsp ground cinnamon

1 tsp ground mixed spice

375ml full-fat milk

165g soft dark brown sugar

1½ tsp bicarbonate of soda

150g unsalted butter, diced

85g black treacle

165g golden syrup

65g stem ginger, chopped

80ml stem ginger syrup

1 egg

This is light years away from the strong, gingery things that gathered dust at your grandparents', wooaaah!

First sift the flour and ground spices into a large bowl. Then pour the milk into a heavy-based saucepan, add the sugar and let it dissolve over a medium heat. Remove from the heat and add the bicarbonate of soda; watch out, it will fizz up a little (better in the pan than in the oven). Leave to one side.

Put the butter, black treacle and golden syrup in a saucepan, place on a medium heat and slowly bring up to a light simmer, until the ingredients have melted and formed a rich syrup. Whisk this mixture into the flour little by little; it will be quite firm to start with but once around half of it is in it will be a bit lighter on the whisk. Then gradually whisk in the milk mixture until smooth. If it is not, whisk a little more; if still not smooth, pass through a sieve. Add the ginger pieces, ginger syrup and egg, give it a good whisk, then leave to rest for a couple of hours.

Pour into a parchment-lined loaf tin about 30cm long, 11cm wide and 7cm deep. Bake at 160°C/Gas Mark 3 for about an hour, until firm to the touch, then turn out onto a cooling rack. Serve warm, with Butterscotch Sauce (see page 372) and Vanilla Ice Cream (see page 382).

RHUBARB CRUMBLE CAKE

To serve six to eight

3 large sticks of rhubarb

50g caster sugar

50g Demerara sugar

grated zest of 1 orange

CAKE MIX

125g soft unsalted butter

125g caster sugar

3 large eggs, lightly beaten

160g self-raising flour, sifted

50ml full-fat milk

CRUMBLE MIX

125g plain flour

95g unsalted butter, cut into small cubes

60g Demerara sugar

30g ground almonds

30g flaked almonds

a pinch of salt

This is having your cake and eating it.

First top and tail the rhubarb, give it a good wash and cut it into slices about 2cm thick. Mix it with the sugars and the orange zest and set aside for 30 minutes.

For the cake mix, cream the butter and sugar together until light and fluffy. Gradually add the beaten eggs, bit by bit to prevent curdling. Then fold in the sifted flour and last of all mix in the milk. Put to one side.

For the crumble mix, sift the flour into a bowl, add the butter and rub them together with your fingertips until they look like large breadcrumbs. Stir in the Demerara sugar, ground almonds, flaked almonds and salt.

Butter a deep 20cm springform cake tin and line the base and sides with baking parchment. Spread the cake mix evenly over the base of the tin, then place the rhubarb on top. Sprinkle the crumble mix over the rhubarb. Place in an oven preheated to 180°C/Gas Mark 4 and bake for about 1½ hours, covering the top loosely with foil if it gets too dark. The cake is ready when a skewer inserted in the centre comes out clean. Serve warm, with custard or extra-thick Jersey cream.

YOU DO NOT HAVE TO USE RHUBARB; YOU COULD USE:
Apples
Apricots
Quinces (you will need to cook them first)
Nectarines
Gooseberries
Pears and ginger
Plums
Damsons

BAKED GOAT'S CURD CHEESECAKE

To serve ten to twelve

1kg goat's curd

juice and grated zest of 2 lemons

7 large eggs

250g caster sugar

1 bottle of Marc de Gewurztraminer d'Alsace

I like the way the recipe says one bottle of marc, taking into account the chef's needs. Cheesecake may have left you uninspired before … Ah! Cheesecakes, they are a-changing.

You will be able to find goat's curd at good cheese shops, such as Neal's Yard Dairy.

Place the goat's curd in a large mixing bowl, add the lemon juice and zest and whisk together with a balloon whisk until light and fluffy. The goat's curd has a tendency to get stuck in the whisk but don't be tempted to use an electric mixer as it will overwork the curd.

Whisk together the eggs and sugar just for a minute, then add them little by little to the goat's curd mixture, whisking constantly. Pour the mixture into a 25cm springform cake tin lined with baking parchment and put it on a baking tray. Place in an oven preheated to 180°C/Gas Mark 4 and bake for about 1 hour, until golden brown. It will still have a good wobble when it comes out of the oven but don't worry, it will set as it cools down.

To serve, cut the cheesecake into slices and pour 1–2 tablespoons of marc over each one.

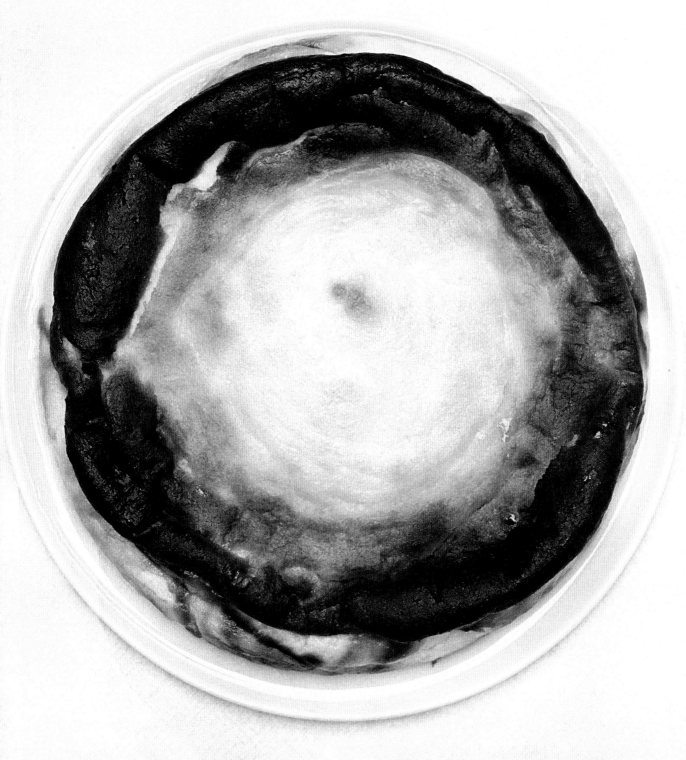

BURNT SHEEP'S MILK YOGHURT
To serve six

10 *large egg yolks*

100g *caster sugar, plus extra for sprinkling*

150ml *full-fat milk*

500ml *sheep's milk yoghurt*

A little musk of farmyard in your pudding.

Place the egg yolks and sugar in a bowl and whisk for about a minute, until well combined. Pour the milk into a saucepan and bring to the boil. Pour the boiling milk over the egg yolk mixture, whisking constantly to prevent curdling. Then add the sheep's milk yoghurt and whisk well.

Pass the mixture through a fine sieve and pour into six ramekins or china moulds. Place them in a roasting tin and pour in enough boiling water to come halfway up the sides of the dishes. Place the tray in an oven preheated to 160°C/Gas Mark 3 and bake for 30–45 minutes, until the custards are set around the sides and still wobble a little in the middle. You must take them out of the oven with the wobble, as the residual heat will finish the cooking. Take the ramekins out of the roasting tin and let them cool for 1 hour, then place in the fridge for 2 hours.

Just before serving, sprinkle caster sugar over the top of the custards – just enough to cover the surface – then caramelize the sugar with a blowtorch or under a grill (a blowtorch gives a better result). Serve on their own or with Shortbread (see page 303).

GOAT'S CURD AND MARC

To serve eight

2 tbsp caster sugar

2 large shots of Marc de Bourgogne
(you can reduce the marc content if
you find it too heady)

675g goat's curd

Goat's curd is available from such places as Neal's Yard Dairy, but if you can't get there a young log of goat's cheese, before it's formed a rind, will suffice.

Stir the sugar into the marc until it has all dissolved (you do not have to apply heat for this) then mix into the goat's curd.

Eat with plain sweet biscuits and/or red fruit.

TREACLE TART

To serve twelve

1.1kg golden syrup (and another 300g up your sleeve)

juice and grated zest of 2 lemons

2 tsp ground ginger

400g white breadcrumbs

PASTRY

315g soft unsalted butter

225g caster sugar

1 large egg

5 large egg yolks

560g strong white flour

You can never have enough treacle.

First make the pastry. Cream the butter and sugar together until white and fluffy. Lightly beat together the egg and egg yolks, then add them to the mixture a little at a time in order to prevent curdling. Sift in the flour and mix until just incorporated. The pastry will be very soft, so wrap it in cling film and leave in the fridge overnight.

Take the pastry out of the fridge and let it soften at room temperature for about 1–2 hours. Then cut it in half and roll out one piece on a lightly floured work surface to about 3mm thick (you won't need the other piece but it will keep well in the freezer). Use to line a 30cm loose-bottomed tart tin and chill for 1–2 hours. Then cover with cling film, fill with baking beans and bake in an oven preheated to 180°C/Gas Mark 4 for about 10 minutes, until golden brown around the edges. Remove the cling film and beans and return the pastry case to the oven until it is a good golden colour all over. Remove from the oven and leave to cool.

For the filling, put the golden syrup, lemon juice and zest and ground ginger in a pan and leave over a medium heat until hot. Stir in the breadcrumbs, remove from the heat and leave for about 10 minutes, until the golden syrup has been absorbed by the crumbs. Then add the extra golden syrup little by little until it starts to bleed out of the breadcrumbs; you might not need to add all the syrup.

Pour the filling into the tart case and bake at 180°C/Gas Mark 4 for 30–45 minutes, until golden brown. Serve with extra-thick Jersey cream.

CUSTARD TART

To serve ten to twelve

½ quantity of Treacle Tart pastry
(see previous page)

10 egg yolks

1 vanilla pod

750ml double cream

95g caster sugar

1 nutmeg

Custardy fragility contained by pastry, the purgatory between liquid and wobbles.

Roll out the pastry on a lightly floured work surface to about 3mm thick and use to line a 30cm loose-bottomed tart tin. Chill for 1–2 hours. Cover the pastry case with cling film, fill with baking beans and lightly fold the cling film over the top of the beans. Bake in an oven preheated to 180°C/Gas Mark 4 until the pastry is golden brown around the edges. Remove the cling film and beans and return the pastry case to the oven until golden brown. Lightly beat one of the egg yolks. As soon as the pastry case comes out of the oven, brush all over the inside with the beaten egg to seal any little holes.

For the filling, slit the vanilla pod lengthways and scrape out the seeds. Put the seeds and pod in a saucepan with the double cream and bring slowly to the boil to infuse the cream with the vanilla. In a large bowl, mix the 9 remaining egg yolks and the sugar together just for a minute with a whisk. Then pour the boiling cream onto the mixture, whisking constantly to prevent curdling. Pass through a fine sieve. If there is lots of froth on top, just spoon it off and discard. Pour the custard mix into the baked pastry case, then grate the nutmeg on top (do not use ready-ground nutmeg). Place carefully in the oven without spilling any of the filling down the sides of the pastry case; if you do, you will end up with soggy pastry, which is a no-no for a custard tart. Bake at 120°C/Gas Mark ½ for about 1 hour, until there is only a small wobble in the centre of the tart. Take out of the oven and place on a cooling rack.

Serve warm or cold and, when in season, with some fresh raspberries.

QUEEN OF PUDDINGS
To serve four to six

60g white breadcrumbs

60g sponge cake crumbs

grated zest of 1 lemon

a pinch of freshly grated nutmeg

190g caster sugar

1 vanilla pod

700ml full-fat milk

30g unsalted butter

4 large eggs, separated

a good dollop of Raspberry Jam
(see page 318)

May I say, this is a very lovely pudding indeed. The way they pipe the meringue on at St. John has the effect of a sea of white bosoms with little brown nipples. This may be to do with my foetid imagination, and not to do with the effect the pastry section is after.

Put the breadcrumbs in a large bowl with the sponge crumbs, lemon zest, nutmeg and 30g of the sugar.

Slit the vanilla pod open lengthways and scrape out the seeds. Place the pod and seeds in a pan with the milk and butter and heat until warm. Pour the milk over the breadcrumb mixture and leave to stand for 15 minutes, then stir in the egg yolks. Pour the mixture into a large ovenproof serving dish and place in a roasting tin half filled with hot water. Bake in an oven preheated to 160°C/Gas Mark 3 for 25–30 minutes, until firm to the touch. Remove from the oven and leave to cool for about 10 minutes.

Meanwhile, whisk the egg whites until they form stiff peaks, then gradually whisk in the remaining sugar.

Spread a very large dollop of raspberry jam over the baked mixture, being careful not to break the surface. You can either pipe the meringue on or just spoon it on top. Bake at 200°C/Gas Mark 6 for 8–10 minutes, until golden brown. Serve piping hot, with pouring cream.

RICE PUDDING WITH MARC AND RAISIN CUSTARD

To serve six

125g unsalted butter

150g caster sugar

200g pudding rice

1.5 litres full-fat milk

300ml double cream

1 vanilla pod

a pinch of salt

MARC AND RAISIN
CUSTARD

150ml full-fat milk

300ml double cream

1 vanilla pod

3 large egg yolks

60g caster sugar

60g raisins soaked in marc
(see page 322)

Rice pudding, custard and marc. Where can we go wrong?

Place the butter and sugar in a large, heavy-based casserole and melt over a medium heat, stirring occasionally. Bring to the boil and let it bubble, without stirring, until it turns into a golden-brown caramel. Add the rice and stir to combine it with the caramel, then add the milk and cream. Once the liquid hits the caramel, the caramel will become hard and stringy. Don't worry; as the liquid heats up, the caramel will melt into it and become smooth again. Slit the vanilla pod open lengthways, scrape out the seeds and add the seeds and pod to the rice, together with the pinch of salt. Bring to the boil and place in an oven preheated to 160°C/Gas Mark 3. Bake for 1½–2 hours, until golden brown on top and thick and creamy.

To make the custard, pour the milk and cream into a saucepan. Slit the vanilla pod open lengthways, scrape out the seeds and add the pod and seeds to the pan. Bring to the boil.

Whisk the egg yolks and sugar together in a bowl. Pour the boiling milk over the egg yolk mixture, whisking constantly to prevent curdling. Then pour it back into the saucepan and cook over a low heat, stirring constantly with a wooden spoon, until it has thickened enough to coat the back of the spoon. Strain through a fine sieve into a bowl and add the soaked raisins.

To serve, spoon the hot rice pudding into deep bowls and pour the custard on top, making sure everyone gets a fair amount of marc-soaked raisins (which are like little pockets of joy).

STEADYING PUDDINGS

BRIGADE PUDDING
APPLE AND BLACKBERRY COBBLER
BLACK CAP
BAKED TREACLE PUDDING
BREAD PUDDING
STICKY DATE PUDDING
GINGERBREAD PUDDING
STEAMED LEMON AND VANILLA SYRUP SPONGE
VICTORIA PUDDING
PRUNE AND SUET PUDDING

BRIGADE PUDDING
To serve eight

MINCEMEAT

3 large quinces, cooked as for
Quince and Prunes (see page 345)

2 Cox apples, peeled,
cored and diced

4 Bramley apples, peeled,
cored and diced

250g fresh minced beef suet

440g raisins

440g currants

440g sultanas

135g chopped candied mixed peel

440g soft dark brown sugar

juice and grated zest of 3 oranges

juice and grated zest of 3 lemons

5 tsp ground mixed spice

2 tsp ground allspice

1 tsp ground mace

2 tsp ground cinnamon

100g slivered almonds

and a nice bottle of Armagnac
up your sleeve

SUET PASTRY

500g self-raising flour

a pinch of salt

250g fresh minced beef suet

250–300ml full-fat milk, warmed

When I stayed the weekend with Tanya and Piers Thompson, she produced this delicious pudding, somewhat reminiscent of a bee's bottom with stripes of suet pastry and mincemeat. As well as being a dab hand at pastry, Tanya is a joy to dance with.

To make the mincemeat, mix together all the ingredients except the Armagnac and place on a large plastic tray. Cover and leave in a cool, dark place (not the fridge) for 2 days, mixing two or three times a day.

Transfer the mixture to a large roasting tray, cover with foil and bake in an oven preheated to 140°C/Gas Mark 1 for around 4–5 hours, until the suet has melted and is bubbling and the mixture has darkened. Remove from the oven and leave to cool, stirring every 10 minutes to make sure the fruit is covered by the fat. This helps to preserve the mincemeat. Finally, when cool, add a very generous slosh of Armagnac (about 300ml). Pot in sterilized jars (see page 317) and seal. It will make about 2kg, so there will be plenty of mincemeat left for making mince pies at Christmas.

For the pastry, sift the flour and salt into a bowl and rub in the minced suet. Pour in 250ml of the milk and mix until a soft dough is formed, adding a little more milk if necessary. Wrap in cling film and leave to rest in the fridge for 1 hour.

Roll out the suet pastry to 1cm thick, then cut it into 5 discs as follows: 7cm diameter, 9cm diameter, 11cm diameter, 13cm diameter and 15cm diameter. Butter and flour a 2 litre pudding basin, then start to assemble the pudding.

First, place the smallest disc of suet pastry at the bottom of the basin. Follow that with a layer of mincemeat 1cm thick, then with the next round of suet pastry and another 1cm-thick layer of mincemeat. Carry on until you reach the top of the basin, finishing with suet pastry. Put a circle of baking parchment on top, then cover the basin with a piece of foil (with a generous pleat in the middle) and secure with string. Put it in a deep roasting tin and pour enough hot water into the tin to come halfway up the sides of the basin.

Steam in an oven preheated to 160°C/Gas Mark 3 for about 2½ hours, until golden brown and bubbling hot (remember to keep the water topped up). Turn out and serve hot, with custard or extra-thick Jersey cream.

APPLE AND BLACKBERRY COBBLER

To serve six

6 Bramley apples, peeled, cored and finely chopped

50g unsalted butter

75g soft light brown sugar

juice and grated zest of 1 lemon

250g blackberries

1 egg, beaten, to glaze

Demerara sugar, for sprinkling

DOUGH

225g self-raising flour

100g unsalted butter, diced

50g caster sugar

juice and grated zest of ½ lemon

1 large egg, lightly beaten

about 50ml full-fat milk

My mum still remembers lying in bed and hearing the sound of the mill workers' clogs on the cobbled streets of Bolton. Excuse me, I digress.

To make the dough, sift the flour into a bowl and rub in the butter with your fingertips until the mixture resembles breadcrumbs. Stir in the sugar, lemon juice and zest, then mix in the beaten egg. Add enough milk to make a soft, pliable dough. Wrap in cling film and leave to rest in the fridge for 3–4 hours.

While the dough rests, make the filling. Put the apples in a saucepan with the butter, sugar, lemon juice and zest and cook over a gentle heat until tender. Remove from the heat and stir in the blackberries. Pour the mixture into a baking dish about 25cm square.

Roll out the dough to 1cm thick and use a pastry cutter to cut out rounds 2cm in diameter. Place them on top of the fruit – they should cover it completely. Brush the top of the cobbler with the beaten egg and sprinkle with Demerara sugar. Place in an oven preheated to 180°C/Gas Mark 4 and bake for about 30 minutes, until the topping is golden brown. Serve hot, with custard or extra-thick Jersey cream.

INSTEAD OF BLACKBERRY AND APPLE YOU COULD USE:
Rhubarb
Pear
Quince
Damson
Gooseberry

BLACK CAP

To serve six

1 quantity of Rice Pudding, left to go cold (see page 363 – omit the custard)

150g tea-soaked prunes (see page 322)

2 tbsp Armagnac

At the risk of repeating myself, come on, rice pudding and prunes. I don't need to spell it out.

Line a 2.3 litre pudding basin with cling film, letting the ends hang over the sides. Drain any excess liquid from the prunes, then place them in the basin and pour the Armagnac over them. Spoon in the cold rice pudding, filling the bowl right to the top, and cover with the overhanging ends of the cling film. Chill for 3–4 hours.

To serve, turn out the Black Cap onto a plate and accompany with custard or pouring cream.

BAKED TREACLE PUDDING

For four people

100g unsalted butter, softened, plus 2 small knobs of butter

100g caster sugar

2 eggs

100g self-raising flour

grated zest of 1 lemon

a pinch of sea salt

6 tbsp golden syrup (I was advised 4 tbsp by those in the know, but that is simply not enough)

The golden syrup can be replaced by jam with equally joyous results.

To start, take one of your knobs of butter and grease a 500ml pudding basin. For the sponge mixture, cream the butter and sugar with a spoon then add one of the eggs. Mix it in gently with 1 dessertspoon of your flour, to prevent the mixture from curdling, then follow with the other egg. Once the eggs, butter and sugar are one, add the lemon zest and fold in the rest of the flour and the salt.

Pour your golden syrup (or jam) into the pudding basin and then put the sponge mixture on top of this. Cover the basin with buttered tinfoil (use knob number two), including a tuck allowing for the expansion of the sponge, then bake in a medium-hot oven for 35–40 minutes. It is done when you can stick a skewer in and pull it out clean.

When cooked, turn it out onto a warmed dish deep enough for the escaping golden syrup (do not worry, this will work). Serve straight away with lots of cream to hand.

BREAD PUDDING
To serve eight

250g stale white bread (e.g. the
Sandwich Loaf on page 289)

65g fresh minced beef suet

130g soft dark brown sugar

20g finely chopped mixed
candied peel

55g raisins

30g currants

25g sultanas

25g Bramley apples, peeled,
cored and diced

1 large egg

1½ tsp ground mixed spice

½ tsp ground allspice

2 tbsp dark rum

15g unsalted butter,
cut into small dice

Demerara sugar, for sprinkling

BUTTERSCOTCH SAUCE

250g caster sugar

600ml double cream

125g unsalted butter,
cut into small dice

Never waste yesterday's bread.

Cut the crusts off the bread, then rip it into small pieces and place
in a bowl. Cover with water and leave to soak for 25 minutes.

Put all the remaining ingredients except the butter and Demerara
sugar in a large bowl and mix with a wooden spoon for 3–4 minutes,
until thoroughly combined. Squeeze all the excess water out of the
soaked bread – come on, a really big squeeze – then add the bread
to the rest of the ingredients. Mix well for another 3–4 minutes. The
mixture will be very wet. Transfer to an ovenproof serving dish, cover
with the pieces of butter and sprinkle Demerara sugar on top. Place
in an oven preheated to 180°C/Gas Mark 4 and bake for 1½ hours,
until golden brown.

Meanwhile, make the butterscotch sauce. Put the sugar into a heavy-
based saucepan with 2 tablespoons of water and melt over a low heat,
tilting the pan occasionally so the sugar melts evenly. Then raise the
heat and cook, without stirring, until it turns into a golden-brown
caramel. Slowly pour in the cream, being careful as the hot caramel
will spit. Turn the heat down low and let the caramel dissolve slowly
into the cream. Remove from the heat and whisk in the butter, a few
pieces at a time. Strain through a fine sieve into a bowl.

Serve your pudding hot, accompanied by Vanilla Ice Cream
(see page 382) and the butterscotch sauce.

STICKY DATE PUDDING

To serve eight

220g stoned dates

1 single espresso

375ml water

1 tsp bicarbonate of soda

65g soft unsalted butter

225g soft dark brown sugar

3 large eggs, lightly beaten

225g plain flour, sifted

Butterscotch Sauce
(see previous page)

Uh huh!

Put the dates, coffee and water in a large saucepan and bring to the boil. Remove from the heat and add the bicarbonate of soda. It will fizz and fizz, but wait until it stops fizzing and then stir everything together. Leave for a couple of hours or ideally overnight in the fridge so the dates can absorb most of the liquid.

Using an electric mixer, cream the butter and sugar together for about 5 minutes, until light and fluffy. Gradually mix in the beaten eggs, then the sifted flour. Add the date mixture. The mix will now be very runny but don't worry, it will set during baking, and produce a very moist sponge.

Pour the sponge mix into a greased 1.7 litre pudding basin; it should be about three-quarters full. Cover the mixture with a circle of baking parchment, then place a piece of foil (with a generous pleat in the middle) over the basin and secure with string. Put the basin in a deep roasting tin and pour enough hot water into the tin to come halfway up the sides of the basin. Steam in an oven preheated to 160°C/Gas Mark 3 for about 1½ hours, until the pudding is well risen and firm to the touch (remember to keep the water topped up).

Turn out into a large serving bowl and pour hot butterscotch sauce over the top. Serve with a generous helping of chilled double cream or Vanilla Ice Cream (see page 382).

GINGERBREAD PUDDING

To serve eight

90g stale white bread

175g plain flour

90g ground almonds

175g fresh minced beef suet

25g baking powder

a pinch of salt

1½ tsp ground ginger

1 tsp ground mixed spice

2 large eggs

175g stem ginger in syrup

2 tbsp grated fresh root ginger

3 tbsp grated apple

180g golden syrup

180g black treacle

150ml full-fat milk

Butterscotch Sauce, to serve
(see page 372)

Remember gingerbread when you were young? Well, forget it, you've just grown up.

Cut the crusts off the bread, then rip it into 2cm pieces and place in a large mixing bowl. Sift the flour over the bread, then add all the rest of the ingredients. Stir together for about 4 minutes until thoroughly combined.

Butter and flour a 2.3 litre pudding basin and spoon in the mixture; the basin should be about three-quarters full. Cover the mixture with a circle of baking parchment, then place a piece of foil (with a generous pleat in the middle) over the basin and secure with string. Put the basin in a deep roasting tin and pour enough hot water into the tin to come halfway up the sides of the basin. Steam in an oven preheated to 160°C/Gas Mark 3 for 1½ hours (remember to keep the water topped up).

Turn out onto a serving dish and cover with hot butterscotch sauce. Serve some Vanilla Ice Cream (see page 382) on the side.

STEAMED LEMON AND VANILLA SYRUP SPONGE

To serve four to six

1 vanilla pod

1 lemon

140g unsalted butter

125g caster sugar

3 eggs, lightly beaten

200g plain flour

1½ tsp baking powder

100–150ml full-fat milk

SYRUP

juice and grated zest of 2 lemons

200g caster sugar

150ml water

Keep the scurvy at bay.

Slit the vanilla pod open lengthways and scrape out the seeds, reserving the pod. Zest the lemon. Cream together the butter, sugar, lemon zest and vanilla seeds until light and fluffy, then gradually add the beaten eggs. Sift in the flour and baking powder and fold in thoroughly. Add enough milk to give a soft dropping consistency, then set aside.

To make the syrup, put the lemon juice and zest in a small saucepan with the sugar, water and the reserved vanilla pod. Heat gently, stirring until the sugar has dissolved, then bring to the boil and simmer until the mixture has a syrupy consistency.

Cut the zested lemon in half widthways and trim off the bottom and top. Place the widest end of one of the lemon halves in a buttered and floured 1.2 litre pudding basin and cover with the syrup, reserving a little for later. Spoon in the sponge mix. Place a round of baking parchment on top, cover the basin with a piece of foil (with a generous pleat in the middle) and secure with string. Put the basin in a deep roasting tin and pour enough hot water into the tin to come halfway up the sides of the basin. Steam in an oven preheated to 160°C/Gas Mark 3 for about 2 hours, until well risen and firm to the touch (remember to keep the water topped up).

Turn out into a large serving bowl and pour the last of the syrup over the top. Serve with double cream.

VICTORIA PUDDING

To serve six

160g unsalted butter

120g caster sugar

40g soft light brown sugar

grated zest of 1 lemon

3 eggs, lightly beaten

240g plain flour

a pinch of salt

10g baking powder

about 100ml full-fat milk

Demerara sugar, for sprinkling

FILLING

12 Victoria plums (nice and ripe), halved and stoned

60g caster sugar

2 tbsp quetsch (plum brandy)

Gastronomically as exciting as a Prince Albert.

For the filling, place the plums and sugar in a saucepan and heat very slowly, just to dissolve the sugar. Remove from the heat, add the quetsch and set aside.

Cream the butter, sugars and lemon zest together until pale and fluffy, then beat in the eggs, adding them little by little to prevent curdling. Sift in the flour, salt and baking powder and fold in thoroughly. Add enough milk to give a mixture that drops reluctantly from the spoon.

Arrange the plums over the base of an ovenproof serving dish about 25cm square. Cover with the sponge mix, then sprinkle Demerara sugar on top. Place in an oven preheated to 180°C/Gas Mark 4 and bake for about 30 minutes, until the pudding is golden brown and a skewer inserted in the centre comes out clean. It will rise quite a lot, so make sure it's not too near the top of the oven. Serve hot, with double cream or custard.

PRUNE AND SUET PUDDING

To serve six

450g *Agen prunes (with the stones in)*

50g *unsalted butter*

150ml *Vieille Prune (plus some more up your sleeve)*

grated zest of 1 lemon

SUET PASTRY

250g *self-raising flour*

a pinch of salt

125g *fresh minced beef suet*

125–150ml *full-fat milk, warmed*

1 *egg, lightly beaten*

A match made in heaven.

Mix all the ingredients for the filling together and leave overnight.

To make the suet pastry, sift the flour and salt into a bowl, then rub in the suet. Pour in 125ml of the milk and mix until a soft dough is formed, adding a little more milk if necessary. Wrap in cling film and leave to rest in the fridge for 1 hour.

Butter and flour a 1.2 litre pudding basin. Roll out two-thirds of the suet pastry to 1cm thick and use to line the pudding basin, leaving plenty overhanging the edge. Fill the basin with the prune mixture and add an extra splash of Vieille Prune for good measure. Roll out the remaining pastry and cut a round that will fit the top of the basin. Use it to cover the filling and brush the edges with beaten egg to seal. Trim off the surplus pastry so there is only 1cm left overhanging. Seal the overhanging pastry and lid together.

Place a round of baking parchment on top of the pastry and then cover the basin with a piece of foil (with a generous pleat in the middle) and secure with a piece of string.

Put the basin in a deep roasting tin and pour enough hot water into the tin to come half way up the sides of the basin. Steam in an oven preheated to 160°C/Gas Mark 3 for about 2½ hours, until golden brown on top and piping hot in the middle (remember to keep the water topped up). Turn out and serve with a generous helping of chilled double cream.

ICE CREAM

VANILLA ICE CREAM
TREACLE TOFFEE ICE CREAM
CHOCOLATE ICE CREAM
RIPPLE ICE CREAM
SULTANA AND MARC ICE CREAM
BROWN BREAD AND ARMAGNAC ICE CREAM
SPICED ICE CREAM
DR HENDERSON ICE CREAM
HONEY AND BRANDY ICE CREAM
BLACKCURRANT LEAF ICE CREAM
BUTTERMILK ICE CREAM
LEMON SORBET

VANILLA ICE CREAM

Makes 1 litre

2 vanilla pods
375ml full-fat milk
450ml double cream
5 large egg yolks
150g caster sugar

Where would we be without it?

Slit the vanilla pods open lengthways and scrape out the seeds. Put the seeds and pods in a heavy-based saucepan with the milk and cream and bring slowly to the boil to infuse the vanilla. Meanwhile, place the egg yolks and sugar in a large bowl and whisk together for a couple of minutes.

Pour the boiling milk over the egg yolk mixture, whisking constantly to prevent curdling, then return the mixture to the saucepan. Cook over a low heat, stirring constantly with a wooden spoon, until it thickens enough to coat the back of the spoon. Pour through a fine sieve into a plastic container and cool down quickly in an ice bath (a large bowl filled with ice cubes is fine). Leave in the fridge overnight, then churn in an ice-cream machine.

TREACLE TOFFEE ICE CREAM

Makes 1 litre

375ml full-fat milk

450ml double cream

5 large egg yolks

125g caster sugar

TREACLE TOFFEE

250g black treacle

250g Demerara sugar

60g unsalted butter

Aah baby, let's slip into something a bit colder.

To make the treacle toffee, place all the ingredients in a deep, heavy-based saucepan and bring slowly to the boil, stirring to dissolve the sugar. Simmer for approximately an hour, until thick and glossy, stirring frequently. Pour the mixture onto an oiled metal tray and leave to cool. Break into small chunks and place them in an airtight container (you'll only need half the toffee for this recipe but the rest will keep well).

Pour the milk and cream into a heavy-based saucepan and bring slowly to the boil. Meanwhile, place the egg yolks and sugar in a large bowl and whisk together for a couple of minutes. Pour in the boiling milk, whisking constantly to prevent curdling, then return the mixture to the saucepan. Cook over a low heat, stirring constantly with a wooden spoon, until the mixture has thickened enough to coat the back of the spoon.

Pour through a fine sieve into a plastic container and whisk in half the treacle toffee until dissolved. Cool down quickly in an ice bath (a large bowl filled with ice cubes is fine), then leave in the fridge overnight. Churn in an ice-cream machine.

CHOCOLATE ICE CREAM

Makes 1 litre

*200g plain chocolate, with at least
70 per cent cocoa solids (we use an
El Rey Venezuelan chocolate called
Apamate, at 73.5 per cent)*

6 large egg yolks

115g caster sugar

500ml full-fat milk

50ml double cream

40g good-quality cocoa powder

CARAMEL

70g caster sugar

75ml wate

**We finally did it, battling with the schizophrenic nature of
chocolate – the sweetness going in one direction, the chocolate
taste in another, plus the chalkiness of bitter chocolate. The battle
left us with the perfect chocolate ice cream. I hope you'll agree.**

Chop the chocolate into small pieces and place in a bowl set over
a pan of simmering water, making sure the water doesn't touch the
base of the bowl. Leave to melt.

Put the egg yolks and caster sugar in a separate bowl and whisk
with an electric beater for about 5 minutes, until the mixture is
thick enough to leave a trail on the surface when the whisk is lifted.

Place the milk, cream and cocoa powder in a heavy-based saucepan
and bring slowly to the boil, whisking occasionally to prevent the
cocoa powder sticking to the bottom of the saucepan. Pour it over
the egg yolk mixture, whisking constantly to prevent curdling. Then
return the mixture to the saucepan and add the melted chocolate.
Cook over a low heat for around 8 minutes, stirring constantly.
Remove from the heat and set aside.

To make the caramel, place the sugar and water in a small, deep,
heavy-based saucepan and bring slowly to the boil, stirring to dissolve
the sugar. Raise the heat and simmer, without stirring, until a very
dark caramel is achieved. Remove from the heat and whisk the hot
caramel into the ice cream base a little at a time.

Pour through a fine sieve into a plastic container, then cool down
quickly in an ice bath (a large bowl filled with ice cubes is fine).
Leave in the fridge for 2 days before churning in an ice-cream
machine. Once churned, leave for 3–4 days before eating. I know
this might prove difficult but it does improve in flavour. Serve with
Hazelnut Biscuits (see page 308) and tea-soaked prunes (see page 322).

RIPPLE ICE CREAM

Makes 1 litre

1 vanilla pod

375ml full-fat milk

450ml double cream

5 large egg yolks

155g caster sugar

about 500g fruit purée, jam or sauce – Raspberry Jam (see page 318) or Butterscotch Sauce (see page 372) work well

Who can resist a ripple?

Slit the vanilla pod open lengthways and scrape out the seeds. Put the seeds and pod in a heavy-based saucepan with the milk and cream and bring slowly to the boil to infuse the vanilla. Meanwhile, place the egg yolks and sugar in a large bowl and whisk together for a couple of minutes.

Pour the boiling milk over the egg yolk mixture, whisking constantly to prevent curdling, then return the mixture to the saucepan. Cook over a low heat, stirring constantly with a wooden spoon, until it thickens enough to coat the back of the spoon.

Pour through a fine sieve into a plastic container and cool down quickly in an ice bath (a large bowl filled with ice cubes is fine). Leave in the fridge overnight, then churn in an ice-cream machine. When it's almost frozen, ripple your chosen flavour through the ice cream.

SULTANA AND MARC ICE CREAM

Makes 1 litre

375ml full-fat milk

450ml double cream

5 large egg yolks

130g caster sugar

100g sultanas soaked in marc
(see page 322)

Ice cream ... Wayhey!

Pour the milk and cream into a heavy-based saucepan and bring slowly to the boil. Meanwhile, put the egg yolks and sugar into a large bowl and whisk together for a couple of minutes. Pour in the boiling milk, whisking constantly to prevent curdling. Then pour the mixture back into the saucepan and return to a low heat. Cook, stirring constantly with a wooden spoon, until the custard thickens enough to coat the back of the spoon; don't let it boil or it will curdle.

Pour the custard through a fine sieve into a plastic container and stir in the sultanas and marc. Cool down quickly in an ice bath (a large bowl filled with ice cubes is fine), then leave in the fridge overnight. Churn in an ice-cream machine.

BROWN BREAD
AND ARMAGNAC
ICE CREAM

Makes 1 litre

250g stale brown bread, crusts cut off

250g caster sugar

4 large egg yolks

600ml double cream

1½ tbsp Armagnac

It's amazing how stale brown bread becomes delicious frozen nuduals.

You will not need an ice-cream machine for this recipe.

Whizz up the bread in a food processor or blender to make crumbs, then spread them out on a baking sheet and toast in an oven preheated to 180°C/Gas Mark 4 until golden brown. Remove from the oven and leave overnight to dry out.

Put 75g of the sugar in a heavy-based saucepan with 2 tablespoons of water and place over a low heat until melted, tilting the pan occasionally so that it melts evenly. Raise the heat and boil without stirring until a dark tan caramel is produced. Stir in the whizzed breadcrumbs and pour the mixture onto an oiled baking tray to cool and set. Blitz to coarse crumbs in the food processor and then put to one side.

Place the egg yolks and the remaining sugar in a large bowl and set it over a saucepan of simmering water, making sure the water is not touching the base of the bowl. Whisk with an electric beater until the mixture has tripled in volume and is very thick and glossy. Remove from the heat and leave to cool slightly.

Meanwhile, whisk the double cream until it forms soft peaks. When the egg yolk mix has cooled, fold in the whipped cream, then fold in the breadcrumbs, followed by the Armagnac. Pour into a plastic container and place in the freezer until set. It's great served with Hot Chocolate Sauce (see page 327).

SPICED ICE CREAM

Makes 2 litres

1 litre double cream

1 litre full-fat milk

1 cinnamon stick, broken in half

2 cloves, crushed

3 allspice berries

2 star anise

½ nutmeg

2 cardamom pods, crushed

½ tsp ground ginger

grated zest of 1 orange

grated zest of ½ lemon

10 egg yolks

500g caster sugar

2 tbsp ruby port

One of Justin's cheeky creations.

Place the cream, milk, spices and fruit zest in a plastic container and leave in the fridge for around 16 hours to infuse. Transfer to a saucepan and bring slowly to the boil. Meanwhile, place the egg yolks and sugar in a large bowl and whisk together for a couple of minutes. Pour the boiling milk over the egg yolk mixture, whisking constantly to prevent curdling, then return the mixture to the saucepan. Cook over a low heat, stirring constantly with a wooden spoon, until it thickens enough to coat the back of the spoon.

Pour the mixture through a fine sieve into a plastic container and cool down quickly in an ice bath (a large bowl filled with ice cubes is fine). Stir in the port. Leave the mixture in the fridge overnight, then churn in an ice-cream machine.

DR HENDERSON
ICE CREAM

Makes 1 litre

500ml full-fat milk

250ml double cream

7 large egg yolks

115g caster sugar

150ml Fernet Branca

40ml crème de menthe

A miracle in the form of ice cream.

Put the milk and cream into a heavy-based saucepan and slowly bring to the boil. Meanwhile, place the egg yolks and sugar in a large bowl and whisk together for a couple of minutes. Pour the boiling milk over the egg yolk mixture, whisking constantly to prevent curdling, then return the mixture to the saucepan. Cook over a low heat, stirring constantly with a wooden spoon, until it thickens enough to coat the back of the spoon. Remove from the heat and stir in the Fernet Branca and crème de menthe.

Pour through a fine sieve into a plastic container and cool down quickly in an ice bath (a large bowl filled with ice cubes is fine). Leave in the fridge overnight, then churn in an ice-cream machine.

HONEY AND BRANDY
ICE CREAM

Makes 1 litre

3 large eggs, separated
125g caster sugar
1½ tbsp pure clear honey
450ml double cream
90ml brandy

Buzzz buzzz.

You don't need an ice-cream machine for this. Basically you make it in three stages, all using an electric mixer with the whisk attachment.

First, whisk the egg yolks, sugar and honey together for 5 minutes on medium speed until pale and fluffy, then put to one side.

Secondly, whisk the cream and brandy together until the cream forms soft peaks, then set aside.

Finally, with a clean whisk, beat the egg whites until they form soft peaks.

With all three stages finished, transfer the egg yolk mixture into a bowl large enough to hold everything. Then fold a quarter of the cream through the egg yolk mix, followed by a quarter of the egg white. Carry on in this way until everything has been mixed together, then pour into a plastic container and freeze overnight.

BLACKCURRANT LEAF ICE CREAM

Makes 1 litre

a handful of blackcurrant leaves
(about 4 or 5)

375ml full-fat milk

450ml double cream

5 large egg yolks

160g caster sugar

A mysterious whisper of blackcurrant.

Rip the blackcurrant leaves and put them in a plastic container with the milk and cream. Leave in the fridge overnight to infuse.

The next day, pour the mixture into a heavy-based saucepan and bring to the boil. Meanwhile, place the egg yolks and sugar in a large bowl and whisk together for a couple of minutes. Pour the boiling milk over the egg yolk mixture, whisking constantly to prevent curdling, then return the mixture to the saucepan. Cook over a low heat, stirring constantly with a wooden spoon, until it thickens enough to coat the back of the spoon.

Pour through a fine sieve into a plastic container and cool down quickly in an ice bath (a large bowl filled with ice cubes is fine). Leave in the fridge overnight, then churn in an ice-cream machine.

BUTTERMILK
ICE CREAM
Makes 1 litre

1 vanilla pod

150ml double cream

125ml full-fat milk

2 eggs

60g caster sugar

60g glucose syrup

500ml buttermilk

50ml Żubrówka Bison vodka

Ice cream with a spring in its step.

Slit the vanilla pod lengthways and scrape out the seeds. Put the seeds and pod into a saucepan with the cream and milk and bring slowly to the boil to infuse them with the vanilla.

In a large bowl, mix the eggs and sugar together just for a minute, then pour the boiling cream over the mixture, whisking constantly. Place the bowl over a pan of simmering water and leave, whisking occasionally, until it reaches 80°C on a sugar thermometer. Then take the bowl off the heat, add the glucose and stir until dissolved. Mix in the buttermilk and vodka, then pass through a fine sieve into a plastic container and cool quickly in an ice bath (a large bowl filled with ice cubes is fine). Refrigerate overnight, then churn in an ice-cream machine.

LEMON SORBET

Makes 750ml

250g caster sugar

375ml water

5 unwaxed lemons

A glass of Russian vodka poured over this will lift everyone's spirits.

Place the sugar and 250ml of the water in a saucepan and bring slowly to the boil, stirring to dissolve the sugar. Simmer until the mixture is reduced to 375ml.

While the syrup is reducing, pare off the zest from the lemons with a vegetable peeler, leaving the white pith behind, then squeeze out the juice. Place the zest and juice in a plastic container, pour over the hot syrup and add the remaining water. Leave to cool, then place in the fridge overnight. Churn in an ice-cream machine.

INDEX

FH
For Brian, Elizabeth, Margot and Annabelle.

JPG
For Louise, my wonderful wife.

ACKNOWLEDGEMENTS

FH

Thank you to all, past and present, at St. John Restaurant, St. John Bread & Wine, St. John Hotel
and St. John Bakery.

JPG

Thank you to all the people I have worked with at St. John Bakery, St. John Restaurant,
St. John Bread & Wine and St. John Hotel – especially Therese Gustafsson,
Luka Mokliak, Fabio Ferreira and Lillie O'Brien.

First published in Great Britain 2012

Text © 2012 by Fergus Henderson and Justin Piers Gellatly
Photography © 2012 by Jason Lowe

The PIG design on the cover and on page 1 is a registered trademark
of St. John Restaurant Company Limited

Bloomsbury Publishing, 50 Bedford Square, London WC1B 3DP

www.bloomsbury.com

BLOOMSBURY and the Diana logo are trademarks of Bloomsbury Publishing Plc

Bloomsbury Publishing, London, Oxford, New Delhi, New York and Sydney

A CIP catalogue record for this book is available from the British Library

ISBN 978 1 4088 0916 7

10 9 8 7

Design: Will Webb
Photography: Jason Lowe

Printed in China by RRD Asia Printing Solutions Limited

All papers used by Bloomsbury Publishing are natural, recyclable products made from
wood grown in well-managed forests. The manufacturing processes conform to the
environmental regulations of the country of origin.

DR HENDERSON

2 parts Fernet Branca

1 part crème de menthe

Ice

Here is a cure for any overindulgence, taught to me by my wise father.

Mix together and drink. Do not be put off by the colour.

Be careful, this is so effective you can find yourself turning to its miraculous powers with increasing regularity. Do not let the cure become the cause.